Francis Thomas Vine

Caesar in Kent

The Landing of Julius Caesar and his Battles with the Ancient Britons

Francis Thomas Vine

Caesar in Kent
The Landing of Julius Caesar and his Battles with the Ancient Britons

ISBN/EAN: 9783744730235

Printed in Europe, USA, Canada, Australia, Japan

Cover: Foto ©ninafisch / pixelio.de

More available books at **www.hansebooks.com**

CÆSAR IN KENT

THE LANDING OF

JULIUS CÆSAR

AND HIS BATTLES WITH THE

ANCIENT BRITONS

WITH SOME ACCOUNT OF EARLY BRITISH TRADE
AND ENTERPRISE

BY THE

REV. FRANCIS T. VINE, B.A.
RECTOR OF EASTINGTON, STONEHOUSE, GLOUCESTERSHIRE

From an Old Print in the British Museum.

TO THE MOST NOBLE

THE MARQUIS CONYNGHAM,

THIS BOOK IS, BY PERMISSION, RESPECTFULLY INSCRIBED

BY HIS LORDSHIP'S CHAPLAIN,

FRANCIS THOMAS VINE.

ERRATA.

Page 14, line 1, *for* "was" *read* "were."

Page 27, line 4, *erase* "other."

Page 51, line 14, *for* "port" *read* "ports."

Page 56, line 21, *for* "him" *read* "Scipio."

Page 56, line 17, *for* "other" *read* "others."

Page 63, line 16, *for* "implies" *read* "imply."

ntry is fable. ythical stories of classic antiquity are chiefly because of the grandeur of the literature which has preserved them, thought worthy of notice and examination; while the Argonautic expedition, the Trojan war, and the story of Romulus and Remus are familiar to every schoolboy, very little effort has been made, at any rate in our own day, to elucidate the truth concerning the somewhat legendary history of what may be called "the heroic age" of our own country. That this history contains the record of brave and noble deeds which, by careful and critical investigation, may be rescued from the region of fable, I have endeavoured in one or two instances to establish

b

PREFACE.

THE early history of every country is more or less mixed with fable. While, however, the mythical stories of classic antiquity are chiefly because of the grandeur of the literature which has preserved them, thought worthy of notice and examination; while the Argonautic expedition, the Trojan war, and the story of Romulus and Remus are familiar to every schoolboy, very little effort has been made, at any rate in our own day, to elucidate the truth concerning the somewhat legendary history of what may be called "the heroic age" of our own country. That this history contains the record of brave and noble deeds which, by careful and critical investigation, may be rescued from the region of fable, I have endeavoured in one or two instances to establish in these pages. My principal object, however, has been to write more fully than has been written before, what has always been regarded as the first page of our country's history, as distinguished from the less reliable traditions of the prehistoric period.

The traces of Julius Cæsar's encampments in the neighbourhood where I lately resided, as Vicar of the parishes of Patrixbourne and Bridge, were first brought to my notice by one who had long made them his study. His love of retirement has prevented him from associating his name with this work; but I desire gratefully to acknowledge the deep interest he has taken in its production, and the important help which he has rendered me throughout its preparation, by giving me the benefit of his archæological researches of many years.

I have sought no novel sites for Cæsar's landing and struggles with our British forefathers. In all cases the only traditions extant corroborate the choice of the localities in which I have placed the scenes of his battles. I believe that where tradition unhesitatingly localises events, it may generally be relied upon. A striking instance of the accuracy with which the memory of events has thus been preserved for many centuries has been made public while these pages have been passing through the press. It occurred in connection with the remarkable discovery by Mr Petrie of the Palace of King Pharaoh at Tahpanhes, in Egypt. When he approached, wearied and footsore, the group of mounds called Tell Defennah, which have long been supposed to be the Tahpanhes of the Bible, "he beheld," as the *Times* article graphically relates, "one of these mounds, consisting of the burnt and blackened ruins of a huge pile of brick buildings, standing high against a lurid sky and reddened by a fiery sunset. His Arabs hastened to tell him its local name; and he may be envied the delightful surprise with which he learnt that it is known far and near as 'El Kasr el Bint el Yahudî'— —the Castle of the Jew's Daughter." This information enabled Mr Petrie to identify this ruined pile with the House in Tahpanhes which, as we gather from the 43rd chapter of the Book of the Prophet Jeremiah, Pharaoh set apart as a residence for the daughters of the Jewish King Zedekiah when he was dethroned and carried captive to Babylon. Thus local tradition has afforded a remarkable corroboration of this seemingly unimportant detail of the Bible narrative.

Having, as I trust, established clearly Cæsar's landing-place and general route of conquest, it has been my aim to enable the reader to realize the actual scenes in which he moved during his stay in Britain. If it be thought presumptuous to assign to particular localities the footprints of the great conqueror, to assert that here his standard was fixed, that there his entrenchments were thrown up, that along this and that road his legions marched, my reply is that my conclusions must be considered as a whole. After laying down on general lines the places where Cæsar landed and fought his battles, I deem it of importance to show that these localities afford evidence of agreement even with the details of his history.

The dedication of this book has been accepted by the representative of a family which has done much to encourage and promote the study of antiquarian pursuits. The successful researches of the late Lord Albert Conyngham, afterwards Lord Londesborough, in the field of archæology, and the liberal and personal support which he gave to many of our learned societies are well known. The valuable collection also of antiquities at Bifrons, the seat of the Marquis Conyngham, testifies to the same interest in the relics of the past by the grandfather and father of the present Lord. It was my privilege, in connection with a friend already mentioned, to whom their discovery was due, to be of some assistance to the late Marquis Conyngham, in opening three large contiguous Tumuli, belonging, as I believe, to the prehistoric period, in Gorsley Wood, on the Bifrons estate. These were found to contain cists of a remarkable character. My account of this exploration, which was carried out at his Lordship's expense, and with the active assistance of his agent, Mr Robert Smith, was published in the 18th volume of the "Archæologia Cantiana." The cists, which are well worth a visit, are still carefully preserved and protected by order of the present Marquis.

Shortly before his death, I had asked permission of the late Lord Conyngham to dedicate this little book to him, and, with the heartiness and kindliness so characteristic of him, he at once acquiesced, saying, " Of course; won't I read it?" For this he was not spared, but his son, the present Marquis Conyngham, has very kindly granted me the same favour which his lamented father had promised.

I have derived much assistance in the preparation of this work from previous publications. My thanks are especially due to Messrs Cassell & Co. for permission kindly given me to make extracts from a work published by them, "The History of Julius Cæsar," by Napoleon III., to the value of which I have borne testimony in the Introduction. I am also indebted to Mr Edward Hayward, of Deal, for allowing me to quote portions of the late Mr Stephen Pritchard's interesting "History of Deal." of which I am glad to hear he contemplates issuing a new edition. I have also made use, in my description of Dover, of "Batcheller's Sketch of Dover." For this I have the permission of Messrs Cuff

Brothers, of Snargate Street, Dover, who have, I am informed, issued, under the title of "Visitor's Guide to Dover," another edition of this useful compendium. To another publication, "The British Kymry," by the late Rev. R. W. Morgan, of Tregynon, I have made frequent reference. I have failed to discover to whom I should express my obligations, but trust that any representatives of his family will accept this acknowledgment of my indebtedness to his valuable work.

EASTINGTON RECTORY, *August 6, 1886.*

INTRODUCTION.

SOURCES OF THE HISTORY.

THE foundation and text-book of every history of Cæsar's invasion of Britain must necessarily be the account given of the event by Cæsar himself. We must not indeed expect that he would give precise geographical information with regard to the countries which he conquered. His history is the "veni, vidi, vici" of the conqueror whose chief aim was to establish the reputation of his army's success. Still it is universally allowed that his details, when he condescends to give details, are wonderfully accurate. His accounts of the manners and customs of the inhabitants of those lands in which his wars were carried on although necessarily incomplete, have been in most particulars corroborated by other historians. His computations of the distances between places, and the times in which those distances were traversed by his army, will bear the closest scrutiny. The officers employed by the Emperor Napoleon III. have verified them wherever the localities visited by Cæsar can be assigned in his Gallic and British Campaigns, and have found them strictly accurate. The value of such corroborative evidence cannot be over-estimated. When an Emperor having at his command the resources to be found in the whole civil administration of a country and in an army of half a million of men, gives the order to compare manuscripts, to explore and excavate fortifications, to measure distances, and in every way to elucidate the history of a particular epoch, the results of such investigations carry with them an authority which could not be derived from the researches of any private individual. The conclusions laid down in the following pages with regard to the site of Cæsar's first inland encampment were in the first instance arrived at independently of Napoleon's suggestions, and before his work on the life of Cæsar was seen, but they are found so entirely to agree with and to supplement the remarks of that distinguished Emperor, that they may almost be regarded as a sequel to his work.

Besides the testimony of Cæsar himself regarding his invasion of this country, we have that of Dion Cassius and Plutarch, as well as a few passing notices of that event in other classic writers, which do not, however, throw much light upon the details of his conquests.

Another source of information, and that of great importance, is afforded by the writings of the British bards and historians. First among these must be mentioned the historic Triads. These are disjointed and fragmentary, but they were certainly transcribed at a very early period, and contain the traditional account of various historical events, amongst others of Cæsar's invasion of Britain. They have never been published collectively in English, but most of them will be found in the Welsh language in "the Myvyrian Archaiology." Those relating to Julius Cæsar and the heroic resistance he met with from the British have been embodied in a valuable work, published some years ago by the Rev. R. W. Morgan of Tregynon, under the title of "The British Kymry, or the Britons of Cambria." A larger work was promised by Mr Morgan, but the author of the present treatise has not been able to ascertain that it was ever published.

In addition to that gathered from the Triads, a British version of the events of Cæsar's progress in Britain may be read in the rather fabulous history of Geoffrey of Monmouth, which seems to have had a common origin with "The Chronicle of Tyssilio," translated from a Welsh manuscript in the Red Book of Hergest, found in the Library of Jesus College, Oxford. It is needless to enter into the controversy as to the genuineness of Geoffrey's history, which he professes to have translated from a manuscript received from Walter, Archdeacon of Oxford. His history, and also the very similar record of Tyssilio, contain evidence of fabrication, and are only valuable so far as they agree with, or may be reconciled with, other more trustworthy accounts. They are not certainly to be wholly rejected, for although embellished with much that is legendary by the ingenious translator, there is every reason to believe that they were founded upon early British annals, upon the first records of the traditional knowledge so carefully preserved and for centuries transmitted orally by the ancient Druids and Bards. The accounts given in these British histories should be critically examined with respect to the several events narrated, and compared with other more authentic records of the same events. If, as will often be found, they do not contradict these, but are evidently independent accounts of the same transactions, their corroborative testimony is of considerable value.

The references to Julius Cæsar's invasion contained in "The History of the Britains" by Nennius, in Henry of Huntington, in the Anglo-Saxon Chronicle, in Beda, and in other later authors, can scarcely be considered as independent testimony, being gathered principally from the Roman authorities before mentioned, and in the case of Henry of Huntingdon to a considerable extent also from the earlier British histories. It has not, therefore, been thought necessary to quote them in the present work, except in one or two instances in which their information seems to have been derived from other sources not now extant.

The author has, however, found much important information in the writings of Camden, Leland, and other early archæologists. These have handed down traditions as to the site of Cæsar's landing, and of his first encounters with the British, and have pointed out the position of earthworks and entrenchments existing in their day, many of which may still be traced, marking the scenes of these battles. He has also been assisted by the traditional knowledge still current in the neighbourhood of these localities, particular scenes of historic interest being in some cases indicated by names known only locally, and handed down from age to age. The topographical position of Cæsar's early battlefields being now discovered, as he believes beyond question, the traditional knowledge of them will be seen to harmonize with the accounts given by classic and early British authors, and not unfrequently to reconcile these when apparently at variance.

CHAPTER I.

EARLY BRITISH COLONIES AND WARLIKE ENTERPRISES.

IT is commonly but erroneously supposed that prior to the coming of Cæsar the isle of Britain was known only by name to the ancients, and that it was peopled by barbarous races, shut out by its inhospitable shores from all intercourse with the rest of the world. To say that such was not the case would be to state only half the truth. The testimony of Cæsar, corroborated as it is by that of many other writers, sufficiently proves that not only had the Gauls and other continental nations frequent communication with Britain for trade and other purposes, but that this country was the centre of their religious culture, and a principal source of their military strength. The author has endeavoured in this and the following chapter to describe the condition of Britain, and the relationship of its inhabitants to the neighbouring peoples at the time when Cæsar invaded its shores. In doing so he has deemed it best to illustrate from other authors what Cæsar has himself related, and to show that his candid acknowledgment of the prowess and resources of his British foemen entirely agrees with the estimate which may be formed of their character from what is known or may be conjectured as to their previous history.

No account of Cæsar's invasion of Britain could be deemed complete without some consideration of the reason which he himself gives for visiting these shores.

His commentaries relate : " Cæsar determined to proceed into Britain because he understood that in almost all the Gallic wars succours had been supplied thence to our enemies." The writer of the commentaries doubtless refers principally to the wars Cæsar had himself carried on in the provinces of Gaul, but his memory may have reverted to the history of other previous wars between the Gauls and Romans, in which British warriors had made their name distinguished and feared. The history of the long-continued struggle between these two rival races, the Romans and the Gauls, carries us back to a period more than 300 years prior to the time of Cæsar. At an earlier period even than this the Gauls had established themselves in the extensive district between the Alps and the Apennines, known as Cisalpine Gaul, but they did not come into collision with the Roman armies till the year B.C. 390, A.U.C. 364. Then it was that under Brennus they inflicted the most serious blow which the Roman power ever sustained by the taking and burning of Rome itself, the capitol alone being saved by the payment of a large ransom.

Livy gives the following account of the first inroads of the Gauls into Italy. He says[1] that in the reign of Tarquinius Priscus (B.C. 616, A.U.C. 138) Ambigatus, King of the Bituriges, the chief people of the Celtæ, finding that part of Gaul

[1] Livy, v. 34.

over-populated, sent forth Bellovisus and Segovisus, his sister's sons, with as many as attached
themselves to them, to whatever settlements the
gods, by augury, might direct. The Hernician,
or Black Forest, fell to Segovisus, the road to
Italy to Bellovisus. The forces of the latter were
derived from the Bituriges, Averni, Senones,
Œqui, Ambarri, Carnutes, and Aulerci. Proceeding over the pathless Alps, uncrossed before
by man, and having defeated an army of Tuscans
near the river Ticin, they encamped in Insubria,
and built a city called Mediolanum (Milan). These
early settlers were followed, says Livy, by the
Cœnomani, and the Saluvii. Then the Boii
and Lingones crossed the Pennine Alps and the
river Po, and drove out the Etrurians and Umbrians from the country. Then, last of all, the
Senones possessed themselves of the countries
between the rivers Montone and Fiumesmo. Of
these various settlers, according to Livy, the
powerful nation of the Gauls was composed, who
at last ventured to assault and capture Rome
itself.

The names of many of these early Gallic settlers

are also given by Polybius,[1] who thus describes their nomadic character: "They dwelt in villages open and without walls, they had few or no moveables, they slept without beds, and their chief employments were husbandry and war, since they were totally ignorant of all other arts and sciences; their substance consisted chiefly in cattle and gold, two commodities which they could easily carry with them whenever by any chance they should be compelled to remove. They not only were masters of the country, but compelled the neighbouring nations to pay them obedience. At length they made war on the Romans, whom, after they had vanquished in battle, together with those who took part with them, they pursued three days together, and took at last the city of Rome itself, all but the capitol."

Plutarch gives a very similar account of the first coming of the Gauls.[2] "Now as touching the Gauls they came (as they say) of the Celtæ, whose country not being able to maintain the multitude of them, they were driven to go and seek other countries to dwell in; and there were

[1] Polybius, vol. i., book 2. [2] Plutarch, "Camillus."

amongst them many thousands of young men fit for service, and good soldiers, but yet more of women and little children. Of these people some of them went towards the North Sea, passing the mountains Riphei, and did dwell in the extreme parts of Europe. Others remained between the mountains Pirinei, and the greatest mountains of the Alps, near unto the Senones, and the Celtorii. There they continued a long time, until they happened at last to taste of the wine which was first brought out of Italy unto them. Which drink they found so good, and were so delighted with it, that suddenly they armed themselves, and taking their wives and children with them, they went directly towards the Alps, to go and seek that country which produced such fruit, judging all other countries in comparison with that to be but wild and barren. . . . They conquered at their first coming all that country which the Thuscans held in old time, beginning at the foot of the mountains, and stretched out in length from one sea unto the other. All that country is well planted with trees, and hath goodly pleasant pastures for beasts and cattle to feed in, and is notably watered with goodly running rivers. There was also at that time eighteen fair great cities in that country, all of them very strong and well seated, as well for to enrich the inhabitants thereof by traffic as to make them to live delicately for pleasure. All these cities the Gauls had won, and had expelled the Thuscans, but this was done long time before." The historian then relates that entering further into Thuscan the Gauls at length laid siege to the city of Clusium, the inhabitants of which besought the intervention of the Romans. The representatives sent by the latter, consisting of three of the most honourable of the house of the Fabians, forgetting their character of ambassadors, and joining in hostilities against the Gauls, were the cause of that invasion of Roman territory which lead to such disastrous results.

There can be no doubt from these accounts that the people who took possession of the northern parts of Italy, and became eventually the conquerors of Rome, were drawn from *all parts of Gaul*, and, were there no other testimony, it might fairly be concluded from this fact, that there were among them British warriors. For

Livy states that some of the earlier settlers in Italy came from the Aulerci, a people who inhabited the district between the Seine and the Loire, the sea coast of which district was known as Armorica. This Armorica was so largely peopled from the Isle of Britain, that Pliny reckons the Britanni or Britons among the maritime people of Gaul, and Dionysius Afer, an early Greek writer, does the same in a passage of which Camden gives the following translation—

> "Near the great pillars of the furthest land
> The old Iberians, haughty souls, command
> Along the continent, where northern seas
> Roll their vast tides, and in cold billows rise;
> Where British nations in long tracts appear,
> And fair-skinned Germans ever famed in war."

That the inhabitants of this district and of the adjacent British isles were conspicuously present in the invading army may be further inferred from the description given by Livy, who represents the attacking force as "an unknown and terrible enemy *from the ocean and utmost verges of the earth*." By this description he would certainly include our British forefathers, since the island of Britain was then the furthest known land, and is so described in a passage of Pausanias. "The Iberi and Celti," he says, "live near an ocean, not a river, but near the farthest sea navigated by man; and this ocean contains the island of the Britons."

The method also of warfare of the invaders, their discordant shouts, the extraordinary size of their men, as well as their unencumbered mode of fighting, although to some extent characteristic of the nation of the Gauls, were especially so of the Britons, and seem to indicate the predominance of the latter, and that the leadership of the invading host was entrusted to one of that nation. With regard to these particulars, Livy[1] gives the following account. "The Clusians," he says, "were terrified both by the number and extraordinary size of the enemy, and withal by the kind of arms they used." He speaks also of their rapid marches, and of the barbarous songs and hideous howlings which made all around them resound with a horrible noise;—so great was the panic caused by these, that when the Roman

[1] Livy, v. 35-55.

soldiers "heard the shouts of the Gauls, which seemed to those who stood next to have been raised from the flank, and to the most remote from their rear. they fled in a body without striking a blow or even returning the enemy's shout." The Gauls when "they entered Rome were heard roaring out their howlings and discordant notes, as they strolled in troops round the city walls." Camillus in addressing the people of Ardea incites them to attack their enemy then foraging in the neighbourhood, by describing them as a people advancing in straggling parties, on whom nature had bestowed enormity of size and impetuosity of courage, rather than firmness of body or constancy of mind; and when acting upon his advice, the Ardeans afterwards surprise and slaughter the enemy, "they were all butchered," says Livy, "without resistance, naked as they were born, and fast asleep."

That the characteristics here given of the invading army were such as might be expected from British even more than from Gaulish warriors, may be gathered from the following quotations from classic authors. "The Britons," says

Strabo, "in stature exceed the Gauls, and their hair is not so yellow nor their bodies so well set. Let this be an argument of their tallness, that I myself have seen at Rome some young men of them taller by half a foot than any other men. Yet their legs were but weak, and the other parts of the body showed them to be not well made or handsome." Tacitus says of the Britons that "they show more heat and fierceness than the Gauls;" Dio Nicæus, that "they run at a great rate;" Cæsar, that "they fight in detachments or small bodies of men at a time, others being ready to relieve them in case of need." Dion Cassius speaks of the loud clamour and songs of defiance with which they advance towards the enemy, and relates that being naked they were able in warfare to swim rivers. Herodian states that they fought "with a sword hanging by their naked bodies." With regard to their simple mode of life, it is described in very similar terms to those in which Polybius described the Gauls who first settled in Italy. Diodorus Siculus[1] gives the following:—" Further, they

[1] Diodor Siculi, Bibliotheca Historica, lib. i. ch. 4.

say that its aboriginal tribes inhabit Britain, in their usages preserving the primitive modes of life; for in their wars they use chariots as the ancient Greek heroes are reported to have done in the Trojan war, and they have mean habitations, constructed for the most part of reeds and of wood, and they gather in their harvest by cutting off the ears of corn and storing them in subterranean repositories: that they cull therefrom daily such as are old, and dressing them have thence their substance: that they are simple in their manners, and far removed from the cunning and wickedness of men of the present day: that their modes of living are frugal, and greatly differing from the luxury consequent on riches." Dion Cassius[1] also makes Bunduica (or Boadicea) say in her address to her army, comparing the Romans with the Britons, "We are endued with courage so superior, that we deem our tents more secure than their walls, and our shields a better defence than their complete armour. If we choose to retreat to any place, we hide ourselves in marshes and mountains,

[1] Dio. Cass., lxii. 5.

where we can neither be discovered nor taken; whereas they, from the weight of their armour, are neither able to pursue others nor to escape themselves: moreover, they stand in so much need of shade and shelter, pounded corn, wine and oil, that if one of these things fail them they perish; while to us every herb and root is food, every juice is oil, every stream is wine, and every tree an house." Strabo again says of the inhabitants of the Cassiterides, by which name some authors seem to refer to the Scilly Isles, others to the British Isles generally, that "they subsist by their cattle, leading for the most part a wandering life." Pomponius Mela says: "The Britons are uncultivated, and in proportion as they live a great distance from the Continent, they are unacquainted with the wealth and riches in other places, theirs consisting wholly in cattle and the extent of their grounds."

This simplicity of life, which Mela and some other writers attributed to ignorance of luxury, was, however, adopted not from necessity but from choice. The Britons and Gauls owed the formation of their national character to the

Druidical religion, which, although a corrupted form of Patriarchal worship, retained nevertheless its primitive simplicity. Hence they despised luxury; and although carrying on a considerable trade with other more cultivated nations, preferred the nomadic life which they had inherited from their forefathers, so that, even when they settled in Italy, they continued, as Polybius states, the same primitive mode of living.

The author has deemed it desirable to show on the testimony of Greek and Latin authors that it is more than probable that British warriors were prominent among the conquerors of Rome; and it may be added that the name of their leader, Brennus, mentioned by Livy, Plutarch, and others, is apparently of British origin. "That Brennus," says Camden, "so famous both in Greek and Latin authors, was a Briton, some think may be easily made out. For my part, I know only thus much in this matter, that the name is not yet quite lost among the Britons, who in their language call a king Brennin."

We need not, however, depend solely upon the classical authorities. That the leader and the dominant part of the invading army were British is distinctly claimed by the British historians. The account of the invasions is as follows:—

Brennus and Belinus, the two sons of Dunwallo Molmutius, King of Britain, disputed after their father's death for the sovereignty of the island. Brennus, after some vicissitudes, being defeated by his brother, took refuge with Seguin, King of the Ligurians of Gaul (called by Geoffry of Monmouth, Seginus, Duke of the Allobroges), a people of Transalpine Gaul. He there became so great a favourite that Seguin gave him his daughter in marriage and bequeathed to him his kingdom. Succeeding to this within a year, he thought himself strong enough to equip an army for the purpose of taking revenge upon his brother Belinus. Marching through Gaul he at length reached Britain, and the two brothers were about to engage in fratricidal strife, when Corwenna, their aged mother, rushed forward in the presence of the armies, and by her entreaties and appeals effected a reconciliation between her sons. Thus united, Brennus and Belinus decided upon the conquest of Europe. They accordingly passed over into Gaul, and in two years reduced all the Celtic population to British rule and administration. Mr Morgan thus describes their conquests: "The Cymro-Celtic army then advanced under the two brothers toward Italy. The Ligurians joined them, and the first military passage of the Alps was, in the face of apparent impossibilities, accomplished. Over the plains of Northern Italy the Kimric army swept in three divisions. The Etrurians made a gallant but ineffectual stand in defence of their empire. Defeated in five engagements they withdrew their population southward, consigning each city as they abandoned it to the flames. The old Umbrian[1] nationality was restored, the liberator and the liberated forming from this period one Federation with equal rights and laws."

After the conquest of Cisalpine Gaul, the

[1] The Umbrians were probably the same nation as the Kimri, the ancient inhabitants of Britain and of some parts of the Continent, whom Camden supposes to have been originally Gomeric (descendants of Gomer, the eldest son of Japhet); others to have been Scythians, the same people as the Cimmerians, a nation from the shores of the Euxine, or Black Sea), and so named by the Greeks from the darkness of their country.

brothers seem to have parted. Belinus marched northwards, and was engaged in subduing the various tribes, known afterwards as the German people, while Brennus extended his conquests southwards, and at length became the conqueror of Rome, demanding and obtaining a ransom of 1000 pounds weight in gold in right of his conquest. " When the gold was being weighed in the presence of the different commanders, Brennus, taking off his belt and sword, threw them into the opposite scale. 'What means that act?' asked the Roman consul. 'It means,' replied Brennus, 'gwae gwaethedigion' (væ victis), woe to the vanquished. The Romans endured the taunt in silence. The gold was transferred to Narbonne in Gaul. Brennus withdrew his troops from Rome, but reigned for thirty years afterwards in Northern Italy."[1] It is probable that he here founded a dynasty, his successors also bearing the name Brennus, as the kings of Egypt were called Pharaoh, and the Roman emperors Cæsar, after the names of the founders of their dynasties. It is at any rate recorded that the chief leader of

[1] Morgan, " Cambrian History."

the Gauls who invaded Macedonia and Greece, B.C. 280-279, was named Brennus.

Now, whatever may be said in general of the credibility of the British historians, it is evident that the account given by them of the invasion of Italy was mainly derived from sources independent of the narrative given by the Roman authors. There is a general similarity between the two stories, but at the same time such divergencies as could only be accounted for by the fact that the British and Roman authors drew their information from different traditional accounts. In both narratives two brothers leave their country together with a numerous host. The Roman authors give their names as Bellovisus and Segovisus, sons of Ambigatus, king of the Bituriges in Gaul. Segovisus seeks the Hernician or Black Forest in Germany; Bellovisus establishes a Gallic colony in Italy, and is succeeded apparently by Brennus, the conqueror of Rome. The British historians, on the other hand, call the brothers Bellinus and Brennus sons of a British sovereign, and say that the latter became the son-in-law of Seginus or Seguin, duke of the Allobroges or

Ligurians of Gaul. Both brothers march to the conquest of Northern Italy, and afterwards separate, Belinus carrying his victorious standard into Germany, Brennus extending his arms further southwards towards Rome. In comparing these two accounts it will be noticed that similar names, evidently originally the same, namely, Bellovisus or Bellinus, and Segovisus or Seginus, occur in both, but their relationship is not the same in the two narratives. Evidently tradition had handed down the names of the heroes and the general complexion of the story regarding them, but, as is usually the case with different traditional accounts of the same event, with considerable variety of detail. Such general agreement, with differences as to particulars, is indicative of the truthfulness and independence of the historian. Had the writers of the British accounts, as some have asserted, constructed a purely fictitious narrative, culling what suited their purpose from the Roman histories, they would have been careful to have avoided such discrepancies as were not necessary to their object. The independence of the British traditional account being thus rendered probable, the statement by the latter that Brennus was a Briton, and that his victorious army comprised, in addition to its Ligurian and other Gallic elements, a considerable proportion of British warriors, may be readily believed, especially as this has been also shown to be probable by the testimony of classical authors.

Nor will it seem unlikely that the army of the Gauls should accept the leadership of a British general, when it is remembered that Britain, as Cæsar tells us, was the centre of the Druidical worship, and as the chief seat of learning was held in such high repute that the youth of Gaul were sent over into Britain to be educated. The leadership in a time of natural danger or adventure falls naturally to that people who have acquired the greatest reputation for bravery, intelligence, and learning.

After the taking of Rome, the British contingent in the army of the Gauls settled partly in Northern Italy, where, according to the account of their incursion by Livy, they had founded the city of Milan, and were probably the same people whom the Roman authors call Insubrians,[1] and partly in the district above the Alps, among the Allobroges or Ligurians, where their leader Brennus had previously occupied the sovereignty. They became here celebrated for their military valour and love of adventure, and were probably the people called Gœsates or Gessates, a name of British origin given them from their custom of serving in the war for pay.[2] Polybius, who relates the history of the wars between the Gauls and the Romans subsequently to the taking of Rome, informs us that after many successful inroads of the former, the tide of war began to turn against

[1] May not the name Insubria have been derived from these British islanders, Ynys in British and Insula in Latin signifying an island? Livy states that the *first* settlement of Gauls was in Insubria, while Plutarch says that the Insubrians were a people derived from the Gauls, clearly indicating that the Gauls, by which term is described the invading host of Gauls and Britons, gave the name to the country in which they settled.

[2] This derivation of the name is given by Polybius, and Camden states " the Britons at this day call their hired servants Guessin." Another reason, however, for the name may be advanced on the authority of Servius Honoratus, who states that the stoutest and most vigorous soldiers were by the ancient Gauls (who spoke the same language as the Britons) called Gessi.

them, and that at length it became necessary for the Gauls to combine in defence of the country which they had made their own. "About 160 years after the capture of Rome, the Bojans and *Insubrians*, the two greatest people of Cisalpine Gaul, sent ambassadors by common consent to *the rest of their nation inhabiting on the other side of the Alps about the Rhone;* these people are called Gessates, from their serving in the war for pay, for so that word properly imports, and prevailing on their two kings Concolitanus and Aneroestus, by means of great sums of money, and by the hopes they gave them of rich booty that would be shared by this enterprise if they succeeded, engaged them to join in a war against the Romans, giving them their faith to assist and abide firmly by them; but the Gessates were not hard to be persuaded. And now, further to incite them, they reminded them of the glory of their ancestors, who had not only vanquished the Romans in battle upon the like expedition, but subdued and became masters of the city itself, and that being lords of all the Romans held, kept their city seven months in possession, and at length, freely and of their own mere motive, restored it to that conquered people as an effect of their generosity, and afterwards returned to their country enriched with infinite booty, without any danger, damage, or impediment. These discourses so animated the leaders of the Gessates, and incited them so powerfully to the war, that it may be said so great an army never marched out from among that nation, nor braver nor more warlike men. . . In the meantime the Gessates having passed the Alps with a magnificent army, furnished with all sorts of arms, came and joined the Cisalpine Gauls, making their rendezvous on the banks of the Po."[1] The forces brought by the Gessates to the assistance of their brethren beyond the Alps consisted of 50,000 foot and 20,000 horse, and *as many chariots.* The use of the latter is worthy of notice, since chariots were not generally employed in war among the *Gauls.* Strabo, on the other hand, says of the *Britons* that " in their wars they make use of chariots for the most part," adding, " as do *some* of the Celti." That

[1] Polyb. vol. i., book 2.

their employment by the latter, however, was very limited is evident from the astonishment expressed by Cæsar at the British chariots, which he could not have felt had he encountered them to any extent in his Gallic wars. It is probable that their use in Gaul was confined to those tribes which were of British extraction, and the fact that the Gessates brought so many of them to the war affords therefore further evidence of their British origin. Polybius further describes the Gessates as a race of giants, and makes their custom of going naked—that is, unencumbered by clothes and armour—into battle the subject of special remark. "These Gessates," he says, "such was their foolhardiness and opinion of their strength, stripping themselves naked, marched in that manner in the front of the battle, with their arms in their hands, conceiving that in that equipage they should not only be able to use their arms with more freedom, but being eased of their garments they should find less impediment from the bushes and briars that might molest them in time of action.

The countenance and behaviour of those who

marched naked at the head of their army was a *sight entirely new;* those giantlike men, strong and well-fashioned, in the prime and strength of their age, where you beheld none in their first ranks who were not adorned with chains, collars, and bracelets of gold."

Thus does the Roman historian trace out the characteristics of that people, who, according to the British account, migrated from our island and settled first in Transalpine, and afterwards in Cisalpine Gaul. In the Insubrians below the Alps, the capital of whose country was Mediolanum (Milan), and in the Gessates above the Alps, in the parts about the Rhone, we recognise the same race, the descendants of those hardy British warriors who made even Rome itself tremble and succumb to their power. We see them 160 years after the taking of Rome, still pre-eminent for their military valour; we find them bearing names of British signification, fighting from chariots as the Britons were accustomed to fight, stripping themselves of their garments after the British manner when going into battle, remarkable for their extraordinary height and imposing appearance, as even their enemies have allowed our British forefathers to have been. Do not these characteristics afford evidence that there existed among the Gauls a people distinct from them although called by their name,—a people separated into two nationalities by the lofty barrier of the Alps, but proud of their common British origin, and united in the time of danger by the memory of that day of triumph when Rome lay in ashes and her proudest citizens prostrate at their feet?

Nor are there wanting proofs of the continued alliance in after years of the Insubrians and Gessates, and further evidence of their British extraction and warlike character.

And first it may be mentioned that Hannibal was careful to secure the aid of these hardy warriors.

"When Hannibal proposed to cross the Alps, he first," writes Polybius,[1] "sent ambassadors to the country at the foot of the Alps and about the River Po, which abounded in brave people given to war; and what was yet more to his wish,

[1] Polybius, vol. ii., book 3.

implacable haters of the Romans ever since the war they made on them. Hannibal then used his utmost diligence, and employed all his forces to advance his purpose; he sent frequent dispatches to the several princes of the Gauls inhabiting on this side the Alps and in the mountains themselves, conceiving it would be a main step towards a happy issue of the war against the Romans to compass his passage through those countries we have named; and after having surmounted the many difficulties of a long march, to be able to engage the Gauls to take part with him and join in the enterprise, as he had laboured to bring it to pass."

Again in Plutarch's history of Marcellus, and his conflicts with the Gauls in the year 212 B.C., we read, "When the Romans had ended their first war against the Carthaginians, which held them fully the space of two and twenty years; immediately after that they began a new war against the Gauls. For the Insubrians, being a people derived from the Gauls, and dwelling at the foot of the Mountains of the Alps on Italy side, being able to make a good power of themselves, did notwithstanding pray aid of the other Gauls inhabiting on the other side of the mountains, and they caused the Gessates, mercenary people and hirelings to them that would give pay, to bring great numbers with them." Peace however at that time was concluded. "But immediately after," says Plutarch, "the Gauls and Gessates renewed the wars again. For there came over the mountains of the Alps 30,000 of them, and they joined with the Insubrians, which were many more in number than themselves." The historian then relates that the united armies laying siege to the city of Acerres, "Britomarus, the king of the Gessates, with 10,000 men went and destroyed all the country above the Po. Marcellus hearing that, marched night and day against the enemy, until he encountered 10,000 Gessates, headed by their king Britomarus, near Clostidium. Having vowed to Jupiter Feretrian to offer him the goodliest spoils of his enemies if he overcame, and seeing Britomarus that he was the goodliest person and strongest of all the Gauls, and that his armour was all gilt and silvered, and so set forth with sundry works and colours that it shined as the sun, he challenged him to single combat. Putting his horse in full career against him, he came with such a force and fury that he pierced his armour with his staff and slew him. After this the Gessates, finding that their king Britomarus was slain, returned back into their own country, and the Insubrians being thus deserted by their allies, their city of Milan was taken by the Romans."

Up to this period, then, the Insubrians and Gessates, although preserving their difference of name, made common cause as one people. In all the Gallic wars they were the leaders, and the name of the King of the Gessates, Britomarus, which, as Camden says, signifies "a great Briton," shows that they had not forgotten their British origin. But they were destined, being now divided, to be dispersed by the advancing power of Rome. Soon after their defeat by Marcellus, Cisalpine Gaul was, in the year B.C. 200, reduced to the form of a Roman province by Scipio Africanus, who, it is said, drove large numbers of the Boii to seek an asylum on the banks of the Danube, where a part of their race had long been settled, as the name implies, in Boihemum (the home of the Boii), now Bohemia. The more warlike spirits among the Insubrians, who had ever been allied with the Boii in their wars against Rome, probably migrated at the same time, or were expelled, either accompanying the Boii into Germany, or joining their brethren, the Gessates, on the other side of the Alps in the parts about the Rhone. The rest of their nation doubtless became merged in the races of Italy. The Gessates in their turn seem to have lost their cohesion as a nation, for their name is heard no more in history. These hardy warriors of the British colonies in Gaul probably found refuge among the Helvetii and other neighbouring peoples, and their continued intercourse with their brethren in Britain enabled first the Helvetii, and then other races of the Gauls in succession, to obtain the valuable assistance which Cæsar says they obtained from these shores.

The Romans, however, were not to be left in undisputed possession of the ground they had gained. The expulsion of the Gauls and their flight to the shores of the Danube and other parts, burning with hatred and desire of revenge, although for a time it freed the Roman people from hostile and troublesome neighbours, was doubtful policy. A century had not elapsed before another immense army of 300,000 fighting men appeared (in B.C. 113) on the confines of the Roman territory below the Danube. They were no longer known as Gauls, but as Cimbri, the generic name of the whole Kimric family, but retained principally by the inhabitants of Northern Germany in the country known as the Cimbric Chersonese, and by the Kymri of Gaul and Britain. They were accompanied by the Teutons and Ambrons, and were joined by some of the Helvetii. The united armies were known as the Celto-Scythian host, and were doubtless drawn from Germany, Gaul, and from the British Isles. From their first appearing in the neighbourhood of the Danube it is probable that they were in the first instance invited by the Boii on the Danube, who had been expelled from Roman territory, and through whose territory they must have passed. They first encountered the Roman armies near

Noreia, where they defeated the Consul, Papirius Carbo. Flushed with success, and scarce distinguishing friends from foes, they became a marauding host, and going into Gaul, ravaged in all directions. Thence returning they defeated three Roman Consular armies in the years B.C. 109, 107, and 105. As yet, however, they did not cross the Alps, but proceeded westward to the conquest of Spain. Afterwards coming back into Gaul (in B.C. 102) they determined upon the invasion of Italy. They divided their forces into two great armies, the Cimbres deciding to pass into Italy through Germany, the Teutons and Ambrons to force a passage through the territory of Genoa against the Roman armies led by Marius. The engagement between the latter opposing forces took place at Aquæ Sextæ (Aix les Bains), where the Teutons and Ambrons were utterly routed, and upwards of 100,000 of them killed and taken prisoners. In this conflict the Ambrons, according to Plutarch, led the battle and were engaged with the Ligurians, who dwelt upon the coast of Genoa. Before they commenced the fight, he says they made a noise simultaneously with their harness,¹ and oft repeated their own name, "Ambrons, Ambrons, Ambrons." The Ligurians, hearing this noise and cry of theirs, plainly understood them, and answered them again with the like noise and cry, "Ligurians, Ligurians, Ligurians," saying that it was the true surname of all their nation. Plutarch suggests that the invaders called out the name of their race either to encourage one another, or to intimidate the Romans with the mere name, reminding them thereby of a victory gained a few years previously, by the Ambrons over the Roman captains, Manlius and Cœpio. It is doubtful, however, whether the Ligurians and Ambrons had ever met in battle before as enemies. The former encounter between the Roman and the Celto-Scythian armies had taken place in the Danubian provinces, where the Ligurians would not be likely to be engaged.

A more probable reason for the remarkable

[1] It seems to have been a custom among the Kymri to endeavour to strike terror by the noise of their chariots. Cæsar says of the British chariot warfare, "This is the kind of fight from chariots: first they ride about everywhere and hurl darts, and generally disorder the ranks by the very terror of the horses, and by the rattle of the wheels."

behaviour of the two contending forces on this occasion may be found in some alliance which had formerly existed between the two races, and the Ambrons in calling out the name of their race, accompanied by their customary method of clashing simultaneously the harness of their chariots, doubtless intended to remind the Ligurians[1] that they were once their brethren in arms, and to induce them to desert to their standard. The Ligurians, however, did not respond in the manner desired. They immediately understood the Ambrons and their intention, but called out in reply the name of their own race, loudly asserting that that was their true patronymic, and thereby rejecting the overtures of their former confreres.

There is some reason to believe that an alliance, if not a relationship, did exist between these two races. Livy states that the Gauls who invaded the country above the Alps did not dispossess the

[1] The origin of this people is involved in some obscurity. They are supposed to be the same people as the Liægrians, called by the Greeks Ligyes and Ligystini. They settled on both sides of the Alps, about the same time that the Umbrians settled in Italy. It is possible that they were of Kymric origin.

Ligurians, but settled by their side, and it will be remembered that according to the British account, Brennus, the British conqueror of Rome, had married the daughter of Seguin, King of the Ligurians, and that when he subsequently invaded Roman territory he was joined by the Ligurians. In espousing the Roman cause the Ligurians were therefore now fighting against their former friends, for the Ambrons, although a people of Germany, and therefore associated in the war with the Teutons, were probably of British origin. From the prominent position assigned to them in the battle they were evidently considered the bravest in the invading army, and as Plutarch states that the most warlike of the Celto-Scythian host dwelt in the farthest parts of the earth near the great forest of Hercynia, it is a reasonable conclusion that the Ambrons were the people who came from this district. Their former alliance with the Ligurians may therefore be easily traced, for it was in this very region that one of the two great divisions of the Celto-British army (namely that under Bellinus) settled after that the two brothers, with the assistance of the Ligurians, had conquered Cisalpine Gaul. That the Ambrons, who, in after years engaged in such deadly conflict with the Ligurians, were descended from these early British settlers in Germany is rendered the more probable by the finding (as related by Camden) at Aix in Provence, where Marius slaughtered the Ambrons, of the coat-armour of the King Beleus on which the words "Belcos Cimbros" were engraven in a strange character. Now the people distinguished in the Celto-Scythian host as Cimbri were not engaged in this battle, but were defeated afterwards by Marius in the *plain of Verselles* under their King Bœorix. The armour therefore could not be that of the King of the Cimbri. But if it be admitted that the Ambrons[1] were also Cimbri, the descendants of the British Umbri or Kymri who conquered Germany under Bellinus, the inscription "Belcos Cimbros" is at once explained. It referred to one of a race of kings who, as the successors of Bellinus, retained his name in an abbreviated or corrupted form.

[1] Strabo mentions the Ambrons with the Tigurini, who were undoubtedly a Celtic or Cimbrian tribe.

After the defeat of the Cimbri and their allies, the Romans were not engaged in any important foreign wars until the time of Cæsar. The hostility of the Gauls, however, was only smouldering, and the Helvetii were preparing a fresh incursion into Roman territory at the time when Cæsar commenced his Gallic campaign. They were the first of the Gauls to feel the weight of his conquering arm. Amongst them, as already stated, the descendants of the ancient British conquerors of Rome probably took refuge when driven back by the advancing power of Rome, and were the means of their obtaining powerful aid against Cæsar from their kindred in Britain. Mr Morgan indeed quotes from the historic Triads an additional reason why a large army was sent against Cæsar at this period from the shores of Britain. "Prior to the campaigns of Cæsar," he says, " in the *north of Gaul* 'the second silver host' recorded in these writings quitted Britain, under the command of Gwenwynwyn and Gwanan, nephews of Caswallon, accompanied by Caswallon in person. They landed to the number of 50,000 men at Brest, B.C. 57.

Marching southward, they effected a junction with the Aquitani. Flûr or Flora, daughter of Mygnach Gôr (the Dwarf), who had been engaged in marriage to Caswallon, had been forcibly carried off by Morchau, a Regulus of Aquitania. The Triads affirm Cæsar to have been the instigator of this act, and the reckless immorality of his private life in Gaul, as depicted by Suetonius, gives colour to the statement. The castle of Morchau was stormed by Caswallon, and Flora brought in safety to Caer Troia (London)." Whatever credence may be given to the details of this account, which seem indeed rather legendary, it was no doubt founded upon a tradition that a considerable army, known as "the second silver host," left the shores of Britain at this period for the purpose of taking part in the desperate resistance which the Gauls were making to the advance of Cæsar. That such was in fact the case, the words of Cæsar himself lead us to believe; nor will his statement that in "almost all the Gallic wars help had been afforded his enemies from Britain," occasion any surprise, since we have been able to trace the existence of a British colony for a period of 500 years on the very confines of Roman territory. A people who retained, as we have seen, British names and characteristics for so long a period, must have continued to hold frequent communication with Britain itself, and it was to be expected that they would seek aid, as doubtless they had done in previous wars, from the mother country. That abundant means of communication existed in the considerable trade carried on between this country and all parts of Gaul, will be fully explained in the next chapter.

CHAPTER II.

THE EARLY TRADE OF BRITAIN.

THE statements of Cæsar with regard to the intercommunication which existed between Britain and the Continent are very conflicting. On the one hand he states that he deemed it of importance, supposing the time of year should fail for his invasion of the country, if only he could approach the island, in order to ascertain what race of men lived there, and to discover its situation, its ports, and means of access, "almost all which things," he says, "were unknown to the Gauls. For neither does any one besides the merchants go there unadvisedly, nor is anything known to the merchants themselves beyond the sea-coast and the parts which are over against Gaul."

Having called these merchants together from every quarter he could not find out from them either the size of the island nor what nations, or how great, inhabited it, nor what was their mode of warfare or form of government, nor even what ports were suitable for a number of large vessels.

On the other hand he speaks of a considerable intercourse between Britain and Belgic Gaul. Colonies from Gaul, he informs us, passed into Britain and established themselves there, bearing the names of the people from which they came. Thus the Atrebates inhabited Berkshire, and Comius, the king of the Atrebates in Gaul, possessed great influence also in Britain. The inhabitants of Wiltshire also were called Belgæ, sufficiently indicating their origin, while Cæsar states that the inhabitants of the southern part of the island by the sea-coast were chiefly of Belgic descent, having crossed over from that country for the sake of plunder and conquest. It is certain that these still kept up intercourse with the Belgæ of the Continent, since Cæsar mentions that, on his conquering the Bellovaci, a Belgic people, he was informed by them that the chief promoters of the war had fled into the isle of Britain. We also learn from the same source that Divitiacus, the king of the Suessiones, having established a very powerful monarchy in Gaul, had also extended his authority into Britain.

Not only had large populations from Gaul migrated to Britain, but there had been a corresponding migration of Britons into Gaul. Besides the British colony in the south of Gaul, the origin and continuance of which we have traced in the previous chapter, the Morini and the inhabitants generally of the district known as Armorica were Britons by descent and association; and this the name itself of the Morini (mor, ynys), signifying "islanders by the sea," seems to imply.

If then there existed this community of interest between the southern part of this island and Gaul, if the inhabitants of these districts were, many of them, of the same race and to some extent under the same rule, how is the statement of Cæsar to be understood that the people of Gaul knew but little of Britain; and that even the merchants who traded there could give no information respecting the country or its principal ports? In reply, we say that there can be no doubt that the ignorance professed by these merchants, and, indeed, by the Gauls generally, was feigned, and that they purposely withheld from Cæsar the information that he sought. Cæsar's narrative of his dealings with the Morini shows that they deceived him in every possible way, as the Britons did afterwards; nor would he be likely to receive from the merchants any information respecting the country whence they derived their trade, but rather every discouragement in his project of invading its shores. For the trade with Britain was most jealously guarded, and the greatest reticence was observed by those who had knowledge of it, as will be shown when we consider what ancient writers relate concerning it. How, we may ask, could there have been this ignorance in Gaul concerning the land of Britain, when Cæsar himself admits that the southern parts of Britain were peopled from Gaul and under the influence to some extent of the Belgic kings; how especially could there have been this ignorance at Boulogne (the Portius Itius), where Cæsar then was, when this port was the British port of the Morini, a people who had migrated from Britain? And if the youth of Gaul went over, as he relates, to Britain for their education, how could the Gauls be ignorant of the race of men and the form of government in that country? If succours were supplied from thence to the Gauls in time of war, how could the latter be ignorant of the customs of war prevailing in Britain? and if the merchants went over thither for purposes of trade, how could they fail to be acquainted with the port and harbours of the British coast? It is indeed a proof of the close tie of kindred and religion which united the two nations, and of how important they deemed it to keep the trade carried on between them from others, that all Cæsar's attempts to elicit information from the Morini and from the merchants were fruitless. From reasons of policy and of kindred, they naturally wished to prevent Cæsar's invasion of the island, and it was therefore to their interest to represent the Britons as savage and barbarous.

and their country as difficult of approach. The same motives, according to Strabo, influenced the Veneti to oppose Cæsar on the ocean. "The Veneti," he says, "who fought against Cæsar by sea were ready to obstruct his passage to Britain, because they used it as a mart." The Veneti of Armorica were the principal maritime people among the Gauls, and the carrying trade between Britain and Gaul was in their hands. As long as the Venetine navy, which was a very powerful one, was mistress of the narrow sea between the two countries, no hostile expedition could quit the ports of Gaul. Before therefore he could invade Britain, Cæsar recognized the necessity of subduing the Veneti. Their very powerful vessels and the superiority of their naval tactics obliged him to take advantage of a dead calm to attack them, when after a battle which lasted from morning till night, they were at last conquered, and to Cæsar's disgrace were sold into slavery.

But it may be asked, what means of intercommunication were there at this early period between Britain and the districts of Gaul more remote from her? Admitting the existence of international relations between Britain and the Belgic states and the district of Armorica, what evidence is there of any intercourse being maintained with the people of the south of Gaul and of those regions which bordered upon the Roman territory? Do not historians inform us that Britain, before the time of Cæsar, was a "terra incognita" to the Romans, who were even doubtful whether it were an island or a continent? In reply to these inquiries it will suffice to examine the accounts which Greek and Roman writers have given. The supposed ignorance of the ancients concerning the British Isles rests chiefly on the authority of Dion Cassius.[1] "To the earliest of the Greeks and Romans," he says, "the existence of Britain was not known, but to those of after times it became matter of dispute whether it were a continent or an island, and much has been written on either side by persons who having neither themselves seen nor heard of it from its inhabitants, knew nothing concerning it, but merely conjectured, as prompted by leisure or the love of controversy: in process of time, however, first under

[1] Dio. Cass., lib. xxxix. 50.

Agricola the Proprætor, and now under the Emperor Severus, it has been clearly proved to be an island." Now this statement of Dion Cassius, who wrote about the year A.D. 230, asserts no more than this: that there was a good deal of random writing by the geographers of a former day about Britain, and that many who wrote were but ill-informed as to its extent and shape, which were not satisfactorily ascertained until the times of Agricola and Severus.

There were, however, several writers of an early period who had obtained reliable information respecting these islands. Even Herodotus, who wrote as early as B.C. 445, states that tin was brought to Greece from the *islands* of the Cassiterides, although he professes to know nothing further about them. Aristotle of Stagira (B.C. 345) also has the following: "The ocean flows round the earth. In this ocean, however, are two *islands*, and those very large, called Bretannic Albion and Ierne, which lie beyond the Celtæ." Polybius of Arcadia (B.C. 130) also refers to the Bretannic *Isles* and the working of tin, but gives no further description of them.

Diodorus Siculus (B.C. 44) says that there "are many *islands* in the ocean, of which that which is called Britain is the largest." Cæsar also distinctly states that Britain is an island, and describes its triangular shape and general characteristics. The statement, therefore, of Dion Cassius that Britain was not certainly ascertained to be an island till the time of Agricola and Severus, is inaccurate, and must be attributed to the conceit, not uncommon in writers of that period, of endeavouring to claim every discovery for their own age, or that immediately preceding.

While, however, it is certain that the best informed historians among the ancients had a general knowledge of the island of Britain, and Pytheas of Massilia (Marseilles) had, about the year 350 B.C., reached it by sea, and having sailed round part of the island travelled homewards by land, it is probable that the Romans in general, notwithstanding the frequent intercourse both for military purposes and for those of trade between the British colony on both sides of the Alps and the mother country, knew but little of it. In the early days of the Roman Republic, literature and learning were held in small repute; so little were they esteemed that Cato expelled the Grecian philosophers from Rome. We cannot, therefore, be surprised if the Romans possessed but a limited knowledge of the history and geography of Britain. The Gauls were only known to them as fierce and barbarous enemies, concerning whom they did not care to enquire. Whatever other races there were amongst them were known all as Gauls, and until the time of Cæsar it is probable that they had a very imperfect knowledge of the British Isles. The trade carried on between this country and the Mediterranean ports, although considerable, was retained exclusively in the hands of Gaulic and Phœnician merchants, especially those of Carthage, a Tyrian colony, and so great was the jealousy lest any other should obtain a knowledge of its source, that Polybius states that none of the people of Massilia could offer anything worthy of remembrance when questioned by him about Britain, neither could those of Narbonne nor of Corbelo, which are the chief cities in that district. Now seeing that Massilia was the principal emporium of the merchants from Britain, there could not have been the ignorance concerning that country which was pretended. The reticence respecting it which Scipio noticed with apparent surprise arose from the same cause which led the merchants who traded with Britain to withhold information from Cæsar.

The accounts of the early commerce between this country and the Mediterranean ports are very interesting, and entirely refute the commonly-received notion that before the coming of the Romans, Britain was inhabited by wild and wholly uncivilized races, who had little intercourse with the people of other lands, and no knowledge or possession of the articles of utility and ornament which were there in use. The nature of this commerce and the means of its transmission are described by several early historians.

The allusions to the trade in tin with Britain by Herodotus and Polybius of Arcadia have been already mentioned. Diodorus Siculus describes it as follows:—"They who dwell near the Promontory of Britain, which is called Bolerium, are singularly fond of strangers, and from their intercourse with foreign merchants, civilized in their habits. These people obtain the tin by skilfully working the soil which produces it: this being rocky, has earthy interstices, in which working the ore and then fusing, they reduce it to metal; and when they have formed it into cubical shapes, they convey it to a certain island lying off Britain, named Ictis; for at the low tides the intervening space being laid dry, they carry thither in waggons the tin in great abundance. A singular circumstance happens with respect to the neighbouring islands between Europe and Britain; for at the high tides the intervening passage being flooded, they seem islands; but at the low tides, the sea retreating and leaving much space dry, they appear peninsulas. From hence the merchants purchase the tin from the natives, and carry it across into Gaul, and finally journeying by land through Gaul for about thirty days, they convey their burdens on horses to the outlet of the river Rhone." In another passage he says, "Above the country of the Lusitanians, there are many mines of tin in the little islands, called Cassiterides, from this circumstance, lying off Iberia in the ocean. And much of it also is carried across from the Bretannic isle to the opposite coast of Gaul, and thence conveyed on horses by the merchants through the intervening Celtic land, to the people of Massilia and to the city called Narbonne."

The following is Strabo's account of the trade with Britain. "And he (Posidonius) says that tin is not found upon the surface, as authors commonly relate, but that it is dug up; and that it is produced both in places among the barbarians who dwell beyond the Lusitanians, and in the islands Cassiterides, and that from the Bretannic isles it is carried to Massilia. The Cassiterides are ten in number, and lie near each other in the ocean, towards the north from the haven of the Artabri; one of them is desert, but the others are inhabited by men in black cloaks, clad in tunics reaching to the feet, and girt about the breast; walking with staves and bearded like goats. They subsist by their cattle, leading for the most part a wandering life. And having metals of tin and lead, these and skins they barter with the merchants for earthenware and salt and brazen vessels. Formerly the Phœnicians alone carried on this traffic from Gadeira, concealing the passage from every one; and when the Romans followed a certain shipmaster that they also might find the mart, the shipmaster of jealousy purposely ran his vessel upon a shoal, and leading on those who followed him into the same destructive disaster, he himself escaped by means of a fragment of the ship, and received from the state the value of the cargo he had lost. But the Romans, nevertheless, making frequent efforts, discovered the passage: and as soon as Publius Crassus, passing over to them, perceived that the metals were dug out at a little depth, and that the men being at peace were already beginning, in consequence of their leisure, to busy themselves about the sea, he pointed out this passage to such as were willing to attempt it, although it was longer than that to Britain."

With regard to the various passages from the Continent to Britain, Strabo writes: "There are four passages commonly used from the Continent to the island, namely, from the mouths of the rivers Rhine, Seine, Loire, and Garonne; but to such as set sail from the ports about the Rhine, the passage is not exactly from its mouths, but from *the Morini* who border on the Menapians, among whom also is situated Itium, which the deified Cæsar used as his naval station when about to pass over to the island."[1]

From the foregoing accounts it would appear that the earliest trade carried on with this country was in the hands of the Phœnicians, who, being at first the principal maritime people, were able to keep the knowledge of it from others for a considerable period, bringing the merchandise by sea through the pillars of Hercules (Straits of Gibraltar), and jealously preventing the ships of other nations from discovering the passage. They received it from the natives, as it would seem, not in Britain itself, but for greater privacy in the islands of the Cassiterides (Scilly Isles).

[1] There was no port nearer the mouth of the Rhine than Itium, in all probability, at the time Strabo wrote. The Morini, that Cæsar might have nothing to conquer, destroyed every building between the Portus Itius and the mouth of the Rhine.

The Greeks at length, and afterwards the Romans, found out the route, and Publius Crassus (perhaps one of Cæsar's generals, see De Bel. Gal., lib. iii. Ch. 7) subsequently made it known. But it is evident that other routes had long been in use, though their existence was before the coming of Cæsar unknown to the Romans, since Strabo speaks but slightingly of that to the Cassiterides as being a much longer route than that to Britain itself, that is, than the ordinary routes between Britain and the Continent.

What were these routes? Strabo says that there were four passages from the Continent to Britain in his time, namely from the mouths of the rivers Rhine, Seine, Loire, and Garonne. It is probable that all these had been used for the purposes of trade before Cæsar's time, but it is certain that one of them had. Diodorus Siculus, in the quotation already given, clearly defines one of these routes. "The people of Bolerium (Cornwall)," he says, "having reduced the tin ore to metal, convey it to a certain island lying off Britain, called Ictis." This they did in waggons at low water. This island is clearly the same as Vectis,[1] originally Ouictis (the Isle of Wight).

[1] It has been contended that the island called Ictis could not have been that now known as the Isle of Wight, since Diodorus is speaking of the trade at the western extremity of Cornwall, from which that island is nearly 200 miles distant. But the similarity of the name Vectis or Ouictis with the Ictis of Diodorus renders it probable that the Isle of Wight is intended. There was no reason why the ore should not have been brought 200 miles by land in order to shorten the sea passage (a dangerous one if from Cornwall) to the Continent. If the merchants conveyed the tin thirty days' journey through the Continent on horses, it was comparatively easy for the Britons to bring it the much shorter distance from Cornwall to the Isle of Wight by the same means of transit; and the words of Diodorus, they "conveyed it *across*" to Gaul, rather implies that they adopted a short passage from Britain to Gaul. The secrecy moreover with which the trade in tin was carried on would compel the miners of Britain if they desired to maintain their relations with both the Phœnician and Massilian merchants to keep from each the knowledge of the trade carried on with the other, so that it would be necessary to negotiate with the merchants from Gaul at some port distant from that at which they sold to the Phœnicians. It is true that the Isle of Wight is not now connected with the mainland at low water as Diodorus says Ictis was. But he also speaks of several islands along the south coast of Britain which were so connected. The only one now connected with the mainland at low water is a very small island, a mere high rock, called St. Michael's Mount, close to Penzance, in every way unsuitable for trading, and *so close* to the mainland that there would have

Here the tin was purchased by the merchants, who, carrying it across to Gaul, either to the mouth of the Seine or to the Portus Itius (Boulogne), conveyed it on horses to the outlet of the River Rhone. From the mention of rivers in connection with the trade routes, there can be no doubt that the merchants used, whenever they could, the water-courses of the rivers for the conveyance of their merchandize. After travelling, as Diodorus relates, for thirty days overland, they would reach in about that time the navigable part of the Rhone, probably near the ancient Lugdunum (Lyons), where the Saone joins the Rhone. Conveying it down this river they would be able speedily to discharge their cargo either at Narbonne or at Massilia (Marseilles), the great emporium of their trade, as both Diodorus and Strabo relate.

been no object in the merchants transacting business there rather than on the mainland itself. It is evident that in consequence of the changes in the coast, several islands, the Isle of Wight included, which once were more or less connected with the southern coast of Britain, have become now wholly separated from it. On the other hand, some which were formerly islands, such as the Isle of Thanet and Richborough (certainly once an island), are now connected with the mainland.

Of the ancient British ports and harbours, there can be no doubt that Dubris (Dover) was the most commodious and most important, being the nearest to the Continent. It was chosen by Cæsar at first as being the most suitable place for landing his vessels on account of its excellent harbour and its readiness of access from the Portus Itius, his place of embarkation. But of this we will treat at greater length in a subsequent chapter. That Itium was a Gallic port, its name "Portus Itius," by which it was known to Cæsar, implies, and its use as such previously to his invasion of Britain may be gathered from the passage of Strabo already quoted : " To such as sail about the Rhine, the passage is not exactly from its mouths, but from the Morini who border on the Menapians, among whom also is situated Itium, which the deified Cæsar used as his naval station when about to pass over to the island." If Cæsar is said to have "used" the port, it is necessarily implied that it was known as a port before his time. With reference to the *routes* which the caravans of merchants adopted in conveying their merchandise across the Continent we have no information, but they were probably those which in after years were defined by the construction of roads. Strabo relates that in the reign of Augustus, Agrippa caused a road to be constructed from Lugdunum (Lyons) to the ocean across the country of the Bellovaci and Ambiani, doubtless the same road which the itinerary of Antoninus traces through Bagacum (Bavay), Pons-Scaldis (Escaut Point), Tournacum (Tournay), Viroviacum (Werwick), Castellum (Cassel), Tarrenna (Théronenne), ending at Gessoriacum (Boulogne). This no doubt indicated the original trade-route which the merchants followed from Lyons to Boulogne, connecting the trade carried on between Marseilles and Britain. The trade routes of a country are not easily diverted, and it is probable that the road made by Agrippa was constructed on the original pathway of the merchant caravans, just as in Britain the Romans formed their vias on the foundations of the former British roads. Another route seems to have been from Boulogne to Bonne on the Rhine. Augustus caused bridges to be thrown over the streams at the time he constructed a road between these towns. The merchants travelling by this route would no doubt avail themselves of the great watercourse of the Rhine, and afterwards of the Rhone, for the conveyance of their wares, but it is doubtful whether the Gaulish merchants made much use of this route, as it would take them through a foreign country rather than through their own.

Having indicated the various centres and sources of the trade between this country and the Mediterranean ports, we will now inquire in what that trade consisted. Of the exports from Britain, tin, the plumbum album of the ancients, was the earliest and most important. It was to procure this that the Phœnician merchants braved a dangerous ocean and the rocky headlands of the islands of the Cassiterides. This was the principal inducement to the merchants of Gaul to undertake their long journeys across the continent between the ocean port and Massilia. Cæsar speaks of tin being found in the southern parts of the island, and iron, although in small quantities, on the sea-coast. The trade of the Phœnicians with Britain in tin must have commenced at least 1400 years before Christ, since tin is enumerated among other metals that passed through the purifying fire in the time of Moses (Numbers xxxi. 22), and is also mentioned by Homer (Iliad, ii. v. 25), and we read of no other country that produced it in any quantity in ancient times except Britain, nor any people who extensively traded in it except the Phœnicians.

An examination, moreover, of the mines of Cornwall affords internal evidence of the remote period at which they were worked, for at the depth of fifty fathoms the miners frequently meet with large timbers still entire, the props and pillars of the mines exhausted at an early age. The earliest name of the country, indeed, is probably derived from the abundance of its wealth in tin, for the Phœnician "Barat-anac," or "land of tin," by which it is said to have been originally distinguished, was afterwards corrupted into Βρετανικη, or Britain, and subsequently, when the Greeks became connected with the trade, this word received the Greek form Cassiterides, from κασσιτερον, a word signifiying tin, in which form it was generally applied to the islands known now as "the Scilly Isles."

When the tin trade commenced with Massilia (Marseilles) by the caravan route through Gaul is not easily ascertained. Massilia was a Greek city founded by the Phoceans of Asia Minor about the year B.C. 600. It soon became a very flourishing city, and continued for some centuries to be one of the most important commercial cities in the ancient world. That its trade with Britain commenced at an early period is certain from the fact that the Greeks obtained their knowledge of Britain from the Massilian merchants about the time of Alexander the Great (*i.e.*, about B.C. 330), and especially from the voyage of Pytheas (of Massilia), who sailed round a great part of the island.

Nor were there wanting other commodities besides tin which the Britons could export. Strabo says that they bartered not only tin and lead (plumbum nigrum), but skins and other articles of commerce. "The country," he says, "produced corn and cattle, and gold and silver, and iron, and also skins and slaves, and dogs sagacious in hunting, which the Celti use for the purposes of war, as well as their native dogs." In these commodities a large trade was doubtless carried on, not only with Marseilles and Phœnicia, but with the Gauls and other neighbouring peoples.

With respect to the foreign produce and manufactures imported into this country in exchange for the tin and other articles of commerce, it is certain that the trade with Phœnicia and Massilia would introduce to the shores of Britain all the wealth of the ancient world. Phœnicia itself produced many articles of superior manufacture. Amongst these may be mentioned the purple-dyed garments of Tyre, the rich tapestry and fine linen wrought in the Phœnician looms. The glass of Sidon, too, made from the fine sand of its sea-shore, was celebrated as the finest and purest in the world, and [1] "the Sidonians had brought its manufacture to such perfection that they were able to impart to it a variety of the most striking and beautiful colours. The artificers also of Tyre were so celebrated even in the time of Solomon, especially in the working of

[1] From Maurice's "Indian Antiquities."

metals and ivory, that they were employed in the adornment of the Temple in Jerusalem and the magnificent palace of Solomon, the one enriched with emblematic devices in cast or sculptured gold, the other with the famous ivory throne inlaid with pure gold, of which the Scripture declares that the like had not been made in any nation. For proof of their great advance in the elegant arts of engraving and sculpture, not less than of their prodigious wealth, we need not go farther than the temple of Hercules in their own city of Tyre, which was not less remarkable for the superb mythological devices, the egg of creation, the nymphœa, and the serpent that adorned its walls, than for those magnificent columns, the one of massy gold, the other consisting of a solid emerald which were seen and described by Herodotus on his visit to that city : the latter of which he asserts by night illuminated the whole of the vast fabric."

Besides the products of Phœnicia itself, its trade with other countries would enable its merchants to barter even the precious metals and stones of India and the East, for the Phœnicians were the general factors of the oriental world ;

all trade being carried on in the earliest times in Phœnician vessels; not indeed that the valuable products of the East would find their way to Britain in any large quantities, but such treasures would probably be thus acquired by the British kings and chieftains. There were, moreover, countries nearer at hand with which the Phœnicians also traded, which could supply articles of exchange such as the Britons would value. With Spain, for example, the Phœnician merchants had carried on an extensive trade at Gades (Cadiz) in gold and silver and brass, even, it is said, before they traded with Britain. The accounts given of the fertility of Spain in gold and silver seem fabulous. Silius Italicus called it the "Aurifera terra," the land that bore gold, and Aristotle[1] informs us that "when the Phœnicians first came among them they found the inhabitants wallowing in gold and silver, and so willing to part with their riches, from their ignorance of the value of those precious metals, that they exchanged their naval commodities for such an immense weight of them, that their ships could

[1] De mirabilibus auscult. Opera, vol. i.

scarcely sustain the loads which they brought away, though they used it for ballast and made their anchors and other implements of silver." These precious metals were carried to Tyre, and thence to the various Mediterranean ports, and transported in large quantities to India and the East by the merchants trading through Palmyra and the Arabian Gulf, though some would doubtless be transmitted to Britain. But gold and silver were not the only products of Spain. Rich veins of copper were also found in its mountains. The making of brass by the fusion of copper with the lapis caluminaris must have been known from the earliest times, since we read early in Genesis that Tubal-Cain was " the instructor of every artificer in brass and iron," and we learn from Homer and other Greek writers that the ancients made of brass their domestic utensils, as well as their arms and accoutrements. That this formed a principal commodity of trade with Britain is undoubted. Cæsar says that "the Britons used *imported* brass," and Strabo that " they bartered tin and lead with the merchants for earthenware and salt and brazen vessels." That they also understood the working of brass is evident from its use in the construction of the tires of their chariot wheels, a specimen of which, dug up by Canon Greenwell in the Yorkshire Wolds, may be seen in the British Museum. Their current coin also consisted either of pieces of brass or of iron rings, whose value was according to their weight. Brass must therefore have been imported in its crude state as well as in the shape of "brazen vessels" as related by Strabo, and accordingly the Phœnician and other merchants would have an article of exchange easily procurable from the neighbouring coast of Spain, and readily received by the Britons in return for the tin and lead which their mines supplied.

Besides the merchandize of other lands introduced by the Phœnician, and we may add by the Greek merchants who at a somewhat later period carried on a traffic with Britain by the same route as the Phœnicians, the Massilian trade would also bring to these shores the art treasures and the products of the skill of almost all nations. Strabo states that earthenware vessels were largely imported into this country in exchange for tin and lead, and it need not surprise us if some of the best specimens of Roman and other pottery found their way to Britain, especially through the Massilian trade. Massilia had cultivated the friendship of Rome long before the coming of Cæsar to our shore, and although she retained her independence as a city, the south-east corner of Gaul, of which she formed a part, had for a considerable time been annexed as a Roman province. Roman earthenware, glass, and other manufactures of that flourishing Republic would therefore be obtainable in Britain through this source, and would be largely distributed throughout the country before the Romans themselves came here. These, however, would naturally consist chiefly of the small articles of commerce. Trinkets, beads, small vessels of glass, pottery, and brass, such articles in fact of feminine ornament and taste as we ourselves are accustomed to barter with the inhabitants of uncivilized countries, would be easily conveyed, and find a ready mart in Britain, and they would be prized in proportion as they contrasted with the rough manufactures of the natives themselves. Such wealth as they could easily carry about with them would alone be valued by a migratory people like the ancient Britons. The simplicity of their habits, their contempt for luxury, and above all the rudeness of their habitations would render all other possession of little use to them. A glance at their dwellings will suffice to show how unsuitable to their wants would have been the articles of luxury and refinement with which the Romans and other cultivated nations were accustomed to adorn their houses. "The number of their oppida (or towns) was great" says Cæsar, and in describing them he states that "the Britons called that a town where they have used to assemble for the sake of avoiding an incursion of enemies, when they have fortified the entangled woods with a rampart and ditch." The remains of many of these oppida may still be seen in almost all parts of the country. In the immediate neighbourhood of Canterbury, the scene of Cæsar's early battles, several may be traced out, namely at Durovernum, Iffin Wood, Atchester Wood, Bridge Hill, and other localities to which reference will be made in the course of this work. They are all similar in form, and answer well to the description given by Cæsar of the British oppida. Some of them are surrounded not by one but by several ramparts with deep ditches between them, and were evidently strongly fortified towns. The habitations contained within these walls of earth were mere huts of wood and thatch, though some which have been discovered consisted of holes dug in the earth, over which a thatched roof was probably constructed. The late Mr Frank Buckland in his "Curiosities of Natural History" thus describes some of them: "The ancient Britons were in the habit of digging holes for shelter. Not many weeks ago some labourers, when digging gravel at Brighthampton, near Oxford, came across several such excavations. They were simply pits dug in the earth large enough to hold one or two persons. From the sides of each of these pits a certain quantity of earth had been removed so as to form a seat. They were in fact nothing more than what were used by the riflemen before Sebastopol in our day. The ancient Britons made them probably only for shelter. At the bottom of these pits were found a few rude arrow heads made of flint, and a quantity of bones. I examined these bones, and found them to be frogs and shrew mice. I suppose that these creatures fell into the pits long after they had ceased to be used by their original makers, and anterior to the time that they were finally filled up." In the remarkable British oppidum at Worlebury, near Weston Super Mare, several circular well-like pits may be seen fairly preserved in shape owing to the rocky nature of the ground in which they have been excavated. One in particular is very perfect, and about two feet from the bottom is a seat formed of the rock, as described in those seen by Mr Buckland, extending all round the pit. Tradition has assigned these circular pits in some parts of the country as the habitations of the Druids. De Moleville in his History of Great Britain says, "There still remain in the western islands of Scotland the foundations of such circular houses capable of containing only one person, and called by the people of the country Druids' houses." It may be observed that in the remains of most British oppida hollows are to be seen which probably were originally of this shape, but owing to the sides having fallen in they have now the appearance of natural hollows in the earth. Some of the larger were perhaps used as repositories for grain and other produce.

A people so primitive in their habits and mode of life would readily supply themselves with all that was necessary for their simple wants. Their food was of the plainest description, consisting principally of milk and the flesh of animals, though in the southern parts of the island they also sowed corn. Their clothing was made of skins. Such earthenware vessels as they required for household purposes they understood the art of making, the rough sun-dried pottery dug up by Canon Greenwell in Yorkshire, by Mr Samuel Carrington in Staffordshire, by Mr Bell in Ilam Wood, and by others, being clearly of native manufacture. Bricks they would scarcely require, except, perhaps, for culinary purposes: but since they made pottery, they could not have been ignorant of the more simple art of brickmaking, especially as it had been practised from the earliest ages of the world, and the materials for it were almost everywhere to be found.

Their weapons of war and agricultural implements they manufactured from the iron found in the country, and from the brass imported from abroad. For smaller vessels of earthenware and brass, for ornaments such as earrings, brooches, and other articles of female decoration, always highly prized, as is the case even in the present day, by nations otherwise uncultivated, they were dependent, as has been already stated, upon the merchants who traded with the country. Nor need it surprise us to find in the graves of these early inhabitants of our soil some of the best specimens of Roman and other art, since Cæsar informs us that where the Druidical religion prevailed funerals were conducted with great expense, and that the surviving relatives were accustomed to bury with the body whatever the deceased person had most prized when living. Considering the large number of articles of foreign manufacture which must have been imported into this country in return for the immense wealth of tin and lead exported by the merchants, it would be strange if we did not find with the remains of our British forefathers valuables of metal and glass and pottery such as they themselves could not produce. And yet, so great is the tendency among archæologists of our day to ignore everything prehistoric, that the discovery of these foreign manufactures is too often regarded as conclusive evidence that the interment of the remains with which they are found took place subsequently to the Roman occupation of Britain. We may well admire and remember with gratitude the higher civilisation introduced into our country by the Romans, and prolonged to some extent during the subsequent Saxon era; but we must not ascribe everything to this period, or forget that it was preceded by a long prehistoric age during which our British ancestors, notwithstanding the primitive mode of life which they followed and preferred, were in frequent communication with foreign nations, and had the means of acquiring the most valuable products of other lands.

CHAPTER III.

CÆSAR'S LANDING-PLACE.

N the two previous chapters some description has been given of the people whom Julius Cæsar assayed to conquer. He had already learned by experience in his Gallic wars that they were a foe not to be despised, but he had yet to experience their indomitable spirit when gathered in defence of their homes, their country, and their gods. He acted, however, with caution. With his usual forethought he took care to obtain as accurate knowledge as possible concerning the country he was about to invade. Not obtaining sufficient information from the merchants who traded with Britain, whom he collected from every quarter, he determined to

send Caius Volusenus by ship to ascertain all that it was possible to discover without disembarking. In this there would be no risk, as since his victory over the Veneti, Cæsar had command of the sea. Having decided, as he naturally would, to invade Britain by the shortest passage from the Continent, he would now be assured by the information gained from Volusenus that this was by the Straits of Dover, and that his nearest port of embarkation was the Portus Itius, now known as Boulogne.[1] Thence therefore he set

[1] That the Portus Itius is Boulogne is argued at some length by the Emperor Napoleon, than whom there can be no greater authority on such a point. After proving that it was at Gessoriacum (Boulogne) that Caligula caused a Pharos to be raised, and that this was also the point of embarkation of Claudius and other conquerors who subsequently crossed over into Britain, affording presumptive evidence of its having been previously used by Julius Cæsar, he points out that the conditions of Cæsar's commentaries are best satisfied by the selection of Boulogne as the place of his embarkation; since first, from thence is the shortest passage from the Continent to Britain, being exactly thirty miles, and secondly, that there is an upper port (Ambleteuse) eight miles distant measured round the coast, where Cæsar's cavalry may well have been detained. "But," says Napoleon, "the peremptory reason why, in our opinion, the port where Cæsar embarked is certainly that of Boulogne is, that it would have been im-

sail, nor can there be any reasonable doubt but that Volusenus, having explored the coast of Britain, would point out to Cæsar the harbour of Dover as *the nearest and most suitable* for the landing of his vessels. That Cæsar actually did seek the shore at this place can however be clearly established from the history.

possible to prepare elsewhere an expedition against England, Boulogne being the only place which united the conditions indispensable for collecting the fleet and embarking the troops. In fact, it required a port capable of containing either eighty transport ships and galleys, as in the first expedition, or 800 ships, as in the second; and extensive enough to allow the ships to approach the banks and embark the troops in a single tide. Now these conditions could only be fulfilled where a river sufficiently deep, flowing into the sea, formed a natural port; and, on the part of the coasts nearest to England we find only at Boulogne a river, the Liane, which presents all these advantages. Moreover it must not be forgotten, that all the coast has been buried in sand. It appears that it is not more than a century and a half that the natural basin of Boulogne has been partly filled; and according to tradition and geological observations, the coast advanced more than two kilomètres, forming two jetties, between which the high tide filled the valley of the Liane to a distance of four kilomètres inland.

" None of the ports situated to the north of Boulogne could serve as the basis of Cæsar's expedition, for none could receive so large a number of vessels, and we cannot suppose that

In determining the direction of his voyage and his place of disembarkation we have this advantage:—that "the commentaries" have given details respecting his *two* voyages to Britain, and expressly state that the points of embarkation and landing were in *each case the same*. They relate that in both expeditions he sailed from the

Cæsar would have left them on the open coast, during more than a month, exposed to the tempests of the ocean, which were so fatal to him on the coasts of Britain.

"Boulogne was the only point of the coast where Cæsar could place in safety his depôts, his supplies, and his spare stores. The heights which command the port offered advantageous positions for establishing camps, and the little river Liane allowed him to bring with ease the timber and provisions he required. At Calais he would have found nothing but flats and marshes, at Wissand nothing but sands, as indicated by the etymology of the word (white sand).

"It is worthy of remark, that the reasons which determined Cæsar to start from Boulogne, were the same which decided the choice of Napoleon I. in 1804. In spite of the difference in the times and in the armies, the nautical and practical conditions had undergone no change. 'The Emperor chose Boulogne,' says M. Thiers, 'because that port had been pointed out as the best point of departure of an expedition directed against England: he chose Boulogne, because its port is formed by the little river Liane, which allowed him, with some labour, to place in safety from 1200 to 1300 vessels.'"

Portus Itius, and that in his second expedition "he sought the same part of the island on which he had learned the previous summer a landing could be best effected."[1] For the purpose therefore of identifying the place of his landing, we can make use of the information given with reference to both his voyages.

In preparation for his first invasion of Britain Cæsar collected eighty transport vessels capable of conveying two legions, and as many galleys as he could obtain: these he placed under the direction of the Quæstor, Lieutenants, and Prefects. Eighteen other transports destined for the cavalry were detained by contrary winds at another port eight miles distant, and were unable to join the rest of the fleet. Cæsar therefore directed the cavalry to proceed thither and to get on board the vessels. Napoleon has no doubt correctly identified this "*farther port*" of Cæsar with Ambleteuse, which is just eight miles from Boulogne. No other port existed within that distance. Calais (Wissand), even now a poor harbour, was probably at that time a

[1] The same fact is also recorded by Dion Cassius, xl. i.

mere marsh, and, even had a port existed there, the Morini and Menapii had probably destroyed every vestige of a building between the Portus Itius and the Rhine before Cæsar's conquest of the country.

Having completed his preparations, Cæsar set sail at the third watch (about midnight) of the night of the 24th August, ordering the transports with the cavalry on board which were detained at Ambleteuse to follow him as *soon as possible*.

The direction he sailed in his first expedition is not mentioned, but it is sufficiently indicated by certain details of the history. For Cæsar tells us, that the eighteen vessels with the cavalry were unable to leave the farther port, owing to contrary winds, till the fourth day after he himself, with the other vessels, arrived at Britain. Now, a glance at the map will show that the wind which kept the vessels in harbour at Ambleteuse must have come from the south or south-west, and the fact that the vessels were detained there for more than four days, shows that it must have been a steady continuous breeze, such as would spread itself over the whole channel. But besides this, even supposing Ambleteuse were not the port of embarkation of the cavalry, the subsequent career of these eighteen vessels shows, that when at length they were able to leave the port they sailed from (whatever it was), they must have proceeded in a northerly, and not a southerly direction, for the commentaries relate, that when they were approaching Britain, and were within sight of Cæsar's naval camp, "so great a tempest suddenly arose, that *none of them could hold its course*, but some were *carried back* to the same place whence they had come forth, others were cast down to the *lower* part of the island, which is *near the sun's setting*, with great peril to themselves." If, then, they were driven by the tempest towards the Cornish coast, that is towards the south-west, in a direction *opposite to* that in which they had been before sailing, it is evident that their course previously was northerly or north-easterly, and the main body of the fleet must, of course, have sailed four days earlier in the same direction. The details, then, of Cæsar's first expedition make it clear that his vessels in sailing to Britain proceeded up channel towards Dover and Deal, and not down channel towards Hythe or Lymne, as some have contended; and that, having started in that direction, there being no change of wind till the fourth day after Cæsar's arrival in Britain, they could not have been diverted from their course.[1]

The account of the second expedition is even more conclusive as to the direction of his sailing. His forces, on this occasion, consisted of five legions and 2000 cavalry. Having provided a sufficient number of vessels for these, " he loosed his ships," the commentaries relate, " at sunset, and having been carried forward by a gentle south-west breeze, the wind being intermitted about midnight, he did not hold his course. Being also carried too far by the tide, at daybreak he beheld Britain forsaken on the *left hand.* Then, again, having followed the change of tide, he strove, by rowing, to gain that part of the island on which he had learned

[1] In confirmation of this statement, that the wind continued to blow from the south-west, Mr Halley has proved that at the time Cæsar set sail from the place where he first approached the shore to his subsequent landing-place with the wind and tide *both* in his favour (as the Commentaries affirm), the tide was flowing *up* channel. His calculation will be given in another page.

the summer before that the landing was best." By the praiseworthy efforts of the rowers, assisted by the tide, he was able to approach Britain with all his vessels about noon.

Now, we have here data from which the course of the invading fleet can be approximately traced. He set sail, we are told, with a gentle, south-west wind at sunset. This favourable breeze continued till midnight, so that, assuming that he left Boulogne about six o'clock, he continued his course with the wind and tide in his favour in a northerly direction for six hours. Now we know something of his rate of speed in his first expedition, and that his ships took about ten hours in crossing over from Boulogne to Britain. In the first six hours then of his second journey, during which the wind continued to blow from the south-west, Cæsar must have accomplished about two-thirds of the passage to the Kentish coast. At midnight, however, the wind slackened or ceased altogether, so that the vessels were carried away by the tide and could not keep their course. They drifted further from the British coast, and at day-break, probably about five A.M.,

Cæsar beheld Britain forsaken on the left hand. It is not likely that in these five hours during which the vessels were acted upon only by the tide they had been carried to any great distance, but the deviation from their proper course caused Cæsar considerable trouble and delay. He took advantage, however, of the change of tide which soon afterwards commenced, and by the extraordinary exertions of his sailors in rowing, was able to reach Britain with all his vessels, transports as well as galleys, by about noon.

Now it will be seen that all the conditions of the narrative are fulfilled if Cæsar be supposed to have landed at Deal (and that *Deal* was his landing-place will in these pages be conclusively established), but how can the supposition of his landing at Hythe or Lymne be entertained consistently with the details of the history? If Cæsar beheld at daybreak Britain *forsaken on the left hand*, he must have been carried during the night a considerable distance above the narrow strip of sea between Dover and Calais, and if this were so, how could his sailors in the seven hours which elapsed between daybreak and noon, even with their most strenuous exertions, have rowed his heavy transports as far south as Lymne or Hythe, a greater distance probably than from Boulogne to Britain, which took him in his first expedition with a favourable wind and tide ten hours.

It is surely then unnecessary to give further consideration to the suggestions, however ably put forward, by Mr Lewin, Mr Beale Post, and others, that Cæsar landed at some place south of Folkstone, since, as has been shown, the details of his two voyages cannot be made to fit in with this theory. Mr Beale Post indeed almost admits that "his wish" to make Cæsar land at Lymne "was father to the thought." "It seems," he says, "an undoubted axiom that if Cæsar's place of arrival is fixed at Dover, and that of his landing at Deal, or the old Richborough Bay, his movements in these parts will never be traced satisfactorily." "On the other hand it is maintained that if Lymne is made the commencing point, research will be attended with very favourable results: that several very remarkable coincidences with Cæsar's narrative can be pointed out; and his battles, marches, and other proceedings, traced with far greater certainty than could be anticipated."

How mistaken Mr Beale Post was in these remarks will be abundantly shown in the course of this volume. Not only can the subsequent movements of Cæsar after his landing at Deal as recorded in history be traced during a considerable part of his progress, but even the scenes of his early battles and encampments can be accurately defined from vestiges of them which in many places yet remain, and from traditions which point them out.

The only other suggestion worthy of notice with regard to the place of Cæsar's landing is that advocated by Archdeacon Battcley, namely, that he landed at Richborough. So much weight attaches to the opinion of this learned author, and so great an interest to the locality of which he writes, that his suggestion and remarks will be considered in a separate chapter.[1]

The necessity of comparing the accounts of Cæsar's two voyages to Britain, in order to ascertain beyond a doubt the direction from the Portus

[1] See Appendix.

Itius which his vessels took on each occasion, has led us into some details of his second expedition. But we will now retrace our steps, and regard Cæsar's approach to these shores after his *first* passage across the channel.

He left Boulogne as has been related about midnight, sailing up the channel, and reached the coast of Britain at the fourth hour of the day (about 10 o'clock A.M.). From the description given, there can be no doubt that he first sought to land at Dover, for Cæsar relates that on approaching the shore he beheld "the armed forces of the enemy posted on all the hills," and that the sea was confined by so close mountains (angustis montibus) that a dart could be hurled from the higher places upon the shore." This description so exactly corresponds with what is known to have been the character of the shore at Dover, that the greater number of writers on this subject, although they have differed considerably as to the place where Cæsar eventually landed, have agreed that it was at Dover that he first sought the shore. And truly when we stand under those overhanging cliffs, whose height towers to heaven, and whose base is washed at high water by the waves, we might fancy that even the Dover of to-day might be the shore described by Cæsar. How greatly then are we strengthened in this opinion, when we are assured that the sea, which is now kept back by the beach and esplanade, formerly swept over the valley where the modern town of Dover is built, reaching the base of the cliffs now known as the western heights, covering the broad space where is now the market-place, and receiving, and at high tide mingling with, the waters of the river Dour, which descend along the Charlton valley, so that literally the sea was, as Cæsar relates, closely confined by mountains. Camden, who published his "Britannia" in the year 1586, thus describes Dover and the interest that belongs to it: "All along from Deal a ridge of high rocks (called by Cicero 'moles magnificæ,' stately cliffs) abounding with samphire, in Latin Crythmos and Sampetra, runs about seven miles to Dover, where it gapes and opens itself to passengers. And the nature of the place answers Cæsar's character of it, receiving and enclosing the sea between two hills. In this break of that ridge of rocks lies Dubris, mentioned by Antoninus, called in Saxon 'Dofra,' and by us 'Dover.' Darellus writes out of Eadmer,[1] that the name was given from its being shut up and hard to come to. 'For,' says he, 'because in old time, the sea making a large harbour in that place spread itself very wide, they were put under the necessity of shutting it up within closer bounds.' But William Lambard, with greater show of probability, fetches the name from Dufyrrha, which in British signifies a steep place. The town, which is seated among the rocks (where the haven itself formerly was while the sea came up farther, as is gathered from the anchors and planks of ships digged up), is more noted for the convenience of its harbour (though it has now but little of that left it) and the passage from thence to France, than either its neatness or populousness. For it is a famous passage; and it was formerly provided by law that no person going out of the kingdom on pilgrimage should take shipping at any other harbour. It is also one of the Cinque ports, and was formerly bound

[1] "The Life of Eadmer," by William of Malmesbury.

to find twenty-one ships for the wars, in the same manner and form as Hastings. On that part which lies towards the ocean, now excluded by the beach, it had a wall, of which there is some part remaining still. It had a church, dedicated to St Martin, founded by Whitred, King of Kent (A.D. 700), and a house of Knights Templars, which is now quite gone; it also affords a seat to the Archbishop of Canterbury's Suffragan, who, when the Archbishop is taken up with more weighty affairs, manages such things as concern good order, but does not meddle in matters of Episcopal jurisdiction. There is a large castle like a little city, with strong fortifications, and a great many towers, which, as it were, threatens the sea under it from a hill, or rather a rock, upon the right hand, that is on every side rugged and steep, but towards the sea rises to a wonderful height. Matthew Paris calls it the key and barre of England. The common people dream of its being built by Julius Cæsar; and I conclude that it was first built by the Romans from those British bricks in the chapel, which they used in their larger sort of buildings."

The notion that Julius Cæsar began to build the castle seems to be derived from a table, or chart, which Camden says was formerly hung up there, which relates that "Cæsar after he had landed at Deal, and had beaten the Britons at Baramdowne (a plain hard by passable for horses, and fit to draw up an army in), began to build Dover Castle, and that Arviragus afterwards fortified it against the Romans and shut up the harbour."

We have quoted in full the remarks of the learned author Camden upon Dover, as they prove the importance which attached to the place 300 years ago, and the traditions respecting its harbour which were then current. The derivations he gives of the name of the place of themselves indicate what its nature formerly was, although it is doubtful whether any of these explanations of its origin is correct, and whether the name "Dover" was not rather derived from the river Dour (meaning "water") which there poured itself into the sea. With regard to the ancient town of Dover, Kilburne says that before King Arviragus stopped up the haven, the town

stretched itself more to the eastward under the castle, but that afterwards it was built on the south-west side. Whether the closing of the harbour was entirely the work of Arviragus seems doubtful. Batcheller in his excellent sketch of Dover says: "What circumstance could occasion so total a change is uncertain; either we must suppose that the old harbour was destroyed, and filled up by design to prevent the entrance of the Romans; or that the sea threw up such a vast quantity of beach, as rendered it impossible for the inhabitants to clear it, and induced them to form a harbour elsewhere which might be less liable to this obstruction." Napoleon gives the following particulars respecting the ancient harbour, and the alterations it has undergone:—
"The port of Dover extended formerly from the site of the present town, between the cliffs which border the valley of the Dour or of Charlton. Indeed from the facts furnished by ancient authors, and geological examination of the ground, it appears certain that once the sea penetrated into the land, and formed a creek which occupied nearly the whole of the valley of Charlton. The

words of Cæsar are thus justified: 'Cujus loci hæc erat natura, atque ita montibus angustis mare continebatur, uti ex locis superioribus in littus telum adjici posset.'

"The proofs of the above assertion result from several facts related in different notices on the town of Dover. It is there said that in 1784 Sir Thomas Hyde Page caused a shaft to be sunk at a hundred yards from the shore, to ascertain the depth of the basin at a remote period. This proved that the ancient bed of the sea had been formerly thirty English feet below the present level of the high tide. In 1826, in sinking a well at a place called *Dolphin Lane*, they found, at a depth of 21 feet, a bed of mud resembling that of the present port, mixed with the bones of animals and fragments of leaves and roots. Similar detritus have been discovered in several parts of the valley. An ancient chronicler, named Darell, relates that 'Wilbred,[1] King of Kent, built in 700 the church of St Martin, the ruins of which are still visible near the market-place, on the spot where formerly ships cast anchor.'

[1] Otherwise called "Withred" or "Whitred."

"The town built under the Emperors Adrian and Septimus Severus occupied a part of the port, which had already been covered with sand, yet the sea still entered a considerable distance inland.

"It would appear to have been about the year 950 that the old port was entirely blocked up with the maritime and fluvial alluvium which had been increasing till our day, and which at different periods have rendered it necessary to construct the dykes and quays which have given the port its present form."

Before this filling up of the harbour there can be no question but that Dofra or Dover (called by the Romans Dubris) was the most convenient and best known port of Britain, and the most frequented by merchants before the coming of the Romans, since it is the nearest point of the shore to the coast of Gaul. Its importance as a military stronghold was fully recognised by the Romans during their occupation of the country. We have no reason, other than that suggested on the chart before referred to, which was formerly hung on the wall of the castle, to believe that Julius Cæsar himself commenced the building of the castle, but part of its fortifications were undoubtedly Roman work. "The Roman fortifications," says Batcheller, "were bounded by the deep ditch, and it will be in vain to search after any military works of the Romans in the castle beyond it. The form of the camp, the ditch, the parapet, and the octagon building all point out the hand of the Roman engineer and the Roman architect. It was no uncommon thing for them, where the ground would admit of it, to make their camp in the form of a parallelogram with the angles rounded off, and to secure it with a deep ditch and a high parapet. This appears to have been the original plan of the Roman camp on this hill before it was altered either by the Saxons or the Romans." Batcheller here refers to the description of a Roman camp given by Hyginus, a writer of the reign of the Emperor Trajan (A.D. 98-117). These Roman works were perhaps due to Aulus Plautius, or more probably to Publius Octavius Scapula, whom the Emperor Claudius sent over in the year A.D. 49, and who, finding the natives inclined to insurrection, disarmed those whom he suspected, and built forts and castles to overawe the rest. The octagon building originally designed for a Roman pharos or lighthouse may be ascribed to the same period. Although therefore there is no sufficient ground for concluding that Julius Cæsar himself built any part of the castle, the early attention given to this work by succeeding Roman Emperors shows how fully they recognized its strategical position and importance.

But to return to Cæsar's narrative. Acting upon the advice of Volusenus, who in his inspection of the coast could not fail to notice the suitableness of this port for a "number of large vessels" such as Cæsar had with him, and perhaps confirmed in his decision by the opinion of Comius the Atrebatian, who was well acquainted with Britain, Cæsar chose Dover as his safest and best port of disembarkation. Had he known the reception that awaited him, he would certainly have chosen differently, but it must be remembered that he had not expected that his landing would be opposed. Ambassadors had come to him in Gaul from many of the British States, bringing in their submission, and so little did he expect a hostile reception, that he entrusted to their hands his faithful ally Comius, who was probably of British extraction, and had great authority both in that country and in Gaul, in order that his persuasions might induce the remaining states to submit to the Roman power. He therefore confidently approached the shore about the fourth hour of the day, that is about ten o'clock in the morning. To his surprise he beheld the armed forces of the enemy drawn up on all the hills; whose darts and other missiles hurled from the high and commanding cliffs at once convinced him of the extreme danger of attempting to land on so confined a shore. A landing, however, must be effected, and that the same day. Cæsar could not without loss of authority submit to the humiliation of returning with all his vessels to the coast of Gaul. Nor could he wait till the next day without affording greater opportunity of resistance to the enemy. He at once summoned Volusenus to his aid. He enquired of him how far the cliffs extended, and whether beyond them the shore offered facilities for a safe landing of his troops. Having ascertained from him that about seven miles farther along the coast there was an open and level shore where he could on more equal terms meet the enemy, he called together the lieutenants and tribunes, and having informed them of what he had learned from Volusenus and of his own plans, he admonished them that his orders should be carried out immediately upon a signal being given (*ad nutum et ad tempus*), since naval matters required rapid and varied movements. Having dismissed them, he waited till about half-past three o'clock, when the tide and wind were both in his favour, and then gave the signal to weigh anchor. Proceeding about seven miles along the shore, and having passed, according to Dion Cassius, "a lofty promontory," which without doubt was "the south foreland," he stationed his vessels "near an open and level shore."

Now if it be admitted that Cæsar set sail from Boulogne and first approached the shore at Dover, it becomes a matter of simple calculation to determine the shore on which he landed. He states that he waited till the tide and wind were at the same time favourable, that is, he waited till about half-past three o'clock in the afternoon ("ad nonam horam"), when the tide had turned and flowed in the same direction as the wind was blowing, and then set sail. Now we have already seen that the wind was blowing up channel in a southerly or south-westerly direction, and that it was a steady continuous breeze which did not change, since it was not till the fourth day after these events that the eighteen transports wind-bound at Ambleteuse were released. Napoleon has given Halley's calculation to show that the tide would also begin to flow in the same direction about half-past three of the 25th August B.C. 55, A.U.C. 699. His argument, which must be considered as a whole, is as follows. He first proves that this was the day on which Cæsar landed. "The *year* of the expedition," he says, "is known by the Consulate of Pompey and Crassus; it was the year A.U.C. 699. The *month* in which the departure took place is known by the following data derived from 'the Commentaries.' The fine season was near its end ('Exiqua pars æstatis reliqua'), the wheat had been reaped everywhere except in one spot ('omni ex reliquis partibus demesso frumento una pars erat reliqua'), the equinox was near at hand ('propinquâ die æquinoctii'). These data point sufficiently clearly to the month of August. Lastly, we have relative to the *day* of landing the following indications:—'After four days past since his arrival in Britain . . . there arose suddenly so violent a tempest.' 'That same night it was full moon, which is the period of the highest tides of the ocean.' ('Post diem quartam. quam est in Britanniam ventum . . . tanta tempestas subito coorta est.' 'Eodem nocte accidit, ut esset luna plena . . . qui dies maritimis æstus maximos in oceano efficere consuevit.') According to this we consider that the tempest took place after four days counted from the day of landing; that the full moon fell on the following night; and lastly, that this period coincided *not* with the highest *tide*, but with the highest *tides* of the ocean. Thus we consider that it would be sufficient for ascertaining the exact day of landing, to take the sixth day which preceded the full moon of the month of August 699; now this phenomenon, according to the astronomical tables, happened on the 31st, towards three o'clock in the morning. On the eve, that is on the 30th, the tempest had occurred. Four days had passed since the landing. This takes us back to the 26th. Cæsar then landed on the 25th of August. Mr Airy, it is true, has interpreted the text altogether differently from our explanation; he believes that the expression 'post diem quartam' may be taken in Latin for 'the third day;' on the other hand he doubts if Cæsar had in his army almanacks by which he could know the exact day of the full moon; lastly, as the highest tide takes place a day and a half after the full moon, he affirms that Cæsar, placing these two phenomena at the same moment, must have been mistaken, either in the day of the full moon or in that of the highest tide; and he concludes from this, that the landing may have taken place on the second, third, or fourth day before the full moon.

"Our reasoning has another basis. Let us first state that at that time the science of astronomy permitted people to know certain epochs of the moon, since, more than a hundred years before, during the war against Perseus, a tribune of the army of Paulus Emilius announced on the previous day to his soldiers an eclipse of the moon, in order to counteract the effect of their superstitious fears. Let us remark also that Cæsar, who subsequently reformed the calendar, was well informed in the astronomical knowledge of his time, already carried to a very high point of advance by Hipparchus, and that he took especial interest in it, since he discovered by means of water clocks, that the nights were shorter in Britain than in Italy. Everything, then, authorises us in the belief that Cæsar, when he embarked for an unknown country, where he might have to make night marches, must have taken precautions for knowing the course of the moon, and furnished himself with calendars. But we have put the question independently of these considerations, by seeking among the days which preceded the full moon of the end of August A.U.C. 699, which was the one in which the shifting of the currents of which Cæsar speaks could have been produced at the hour indicated in the commentaries.

"Supposing then the fleet of Cæsar at anchor at a distance of half a mile opposite Dover, as it experienced the effect of the shifting of the currents towards half-past three in the afternoon, the question becomes reduced to that of determining the day of the end of the month of August when this phenomena took place at the above hour. We know that in the Channel the sea produces, in rising and falling, two alternate currents, one directed from the west to the east called flux (flot), or current of the rising tide; the other directed from the east to the west named reflux (jusant), or current of the falling tide. In the sea opposite Dover, at a distance of half a mile from the coast, the flux begins usually to be sensible two hours before high tide at Dover, and the reflux four hours after.

"So that, if we find a day before the full moon of the 31st August 699, on which it was high tide at Dover, either at half-past five in the afternoon or at mid-day, that will be the day of landing; and further, we shall know whether the current carried Cæsar towards the east or towards the west. Now we may admit, according to astronomical data, that the tides of the days which preceded the full moon of the 31st August 699 were sensibly the same as those of the days which preceded the full moon of the 4th of September 1857; and as it was the sixth day before the full moon of the 4th of September 1857, that it was high tide at Dover towards half-past five in the afternoon (see the Annuaire des Marées des Côtes de France for the year 1857), we are led to conclude that the same phenomenon was produced also at Dover on the sixth day before the 31st of August 699; and that it was on the 25th of August that Cæsar arrived in Britain, his fleet being carried forward by the current of the rising tide. This last conclusion, by obliging us to seek the point of landing to the north of Dover, constitutes the strongest theoretic presumption in favour of Deal."

Now it may be, and has been objected that an argument based upon astronomical calculations relating to the state of the tides more than nineteen centuries ago, cannot carry much weight.

This opinion, however, will not be hazarded by any who know the accuracy with which modern astronomers are accustomed to arrive at results. Nor has another objection which may be urged, namely, that the changes of the coast of Britain may have produced an alteration in the tides, any real importance. The change of coast line would certainly affect the direction of the currents of the ocean, but it would have no appreciable effect upon the tides. As a matter of fact, a change in the shore is continually going on, and the sand banks are continually shifting without causing any alteration of the tides.[1]

---

[1] In corroboration of this the following incident, of which the author has been informed on good authority, may be mentioned. Some twenty-six years ago the authorities of the Trinity House instituted an examination with regard to the position of the various buoys which had been placed on the margin of the sands round the south-eastern coast, especially of the Goodwin Sands. It so happened that a senior pilot of Dover, who in his youth had been present when the buoys were originally placed, was summoned to attend also on this occasion, as he had been the principal cause of attention being drawn to this subject. The result of the enquiry was stated by him to be as follows. The sands had increased so much

Napoleon's lucid argument respecting the direction of the tide when Cæsar quitted Dover has been introduced because it helps to *confirm* the statement that he sailed from thence in the direction of Deal. But, as has been already seen, it is not *necessary* for the establishment of this fact, the other data connected with both his first and second expedition clearly proving that he sailed in a northerly direction.

It remains then only to show that Deal answers to Cæsar's account of his landing-place both in respect to its distance from Dover, and in respect to his description of its shore. We again transcribe from Napoleon's narrative a description of the coast and its suitableness for the landing of troops, as viewed from a military point of view.

"The cliffs which border the coasts of England towards the southern part of the county of Kent

towards the shore that the buoys had to be removed more than a quarter of a mile, to be placed in a depth of water equal to that in which they had originally been fixed. These changes, although they may have produced some variations in the direction of the currents, have made no alteration in the tides, the tables for calculating which, can still be confidently relied upon for accuracy.

form from Folkestone to the castle of Walmer a vast quarter of a circle, convex towards the sea, abrupt on nearly all points; they present several bays or creeks as at Folkestone, at Dover, at St Margarets, and at Oldstairs, and, diminishing by degrees in elevation, terminate in the castle of Walmer. From this point, proceeding towards the north, the coast is flat and favourable for landing to an extent of several leagues.

"The country situated to the west of Walmer and Deal is itself flat as far as the view can reach, or presents only gentle undulations of ground. We may add that it produces, in great quantities, wheat of excellent quality, and that the nature of the soil leads us to believe that it was the same at a remote period. These different conditions rendered the shore of Walmer and Deal the best place of landing for the Roman army.

"Its situation, moreover, agrees fully with the narrative of 'the Commentaries.' In the first expedition, the Roman fleet starting from the cliffs of Dover, and doubling the point of the South Foreland, may have made the passage of seven miles in an hour. It would thus have come to anchor opposite the present village of Walmer. The Britons, starting from Dover, might have made a march of eight kilomètres quickly enough to oppose the landing of the Romans.

"The combat which followed was certainly fought on that part of the shore which extends from Walmer Castle to Deal. At present the whole of this coast is covered with buildings, so that it is impossible to say what was its exact form nineteen centuries ago, but from a view of the locality we can understand without difficulty the different circumstances of the combat described in book iv. of 'the Commentaries.'"

Thus far we have been guided only by the description which Cæsar himself has given of his voyage and disembarkation, and we have been led to Deal as the only place of landing which accords with that description. Let us now see how this selection is corroborated by other evidence.

First, there is the direct testimony of the ancient table (or chart) mentioned by Camden, which formerly hung up in the Castle of Dover, that Cæsar did actually land at Deal, and afterwards defeated the Britons on Baram Downe.

The date of this document is not known, but since Camden, who published his "Britannia" in 1586, says that it had then disappeared from the castle walls, but was preserved in some papers in which it had been transcribed, it must have been of very great antiquity.

Nennius, also a very ancient writer, places Cæsar's landing at Deal, if the passage "Cæsar ad Dole bellum pugnavit" (Cæsar fought a battle at Dole) is correctly transcribed, of which there seems some doubt. But Leland certainly accords to Deal this honour in his Cygnæa Cantio, in which he says—

> "Jactat Dela novas celebris arces,
> Notus Cæsariis locus trophæis."

which Camden thus translates—

> "And lofty Dele's proud towers are shown
> Where Cæsar's trophies grace the town."

With regard to the remains of Roman entrenchments in this place Camden says:—"Just upon this shore are ridges for a long way together like so many rampires, which some suppose the wind has swept together. But I fancy it has been a fence, or rather a station or sort of *ship-*

camp, which Cæsar was ten days and as many nights in making, to draw into it his shattered ships, and so secure them both against tempests and also against the Britons, who made some attempt upon them, but without success. For I am told that the inhabitants call this rampire Rome's work, as if one should say, 'the work of the Romans.'" It may be that in this description of "ridges supposed by some to have been thrown up by the wind," Camden is referring to the sandhills which stretch from Sandown Castle to Pegwell Bay, and of which Mr Pritchard, a local author, has given the following interesting account in his "History of Deal":—"The mounds of sand that abound in Deal it is presumed are all artificial, and thrown up by manual labour. The encroachment of the sea of late years has brought the sandbanks much nearer the sea than formerly. For ages there existed, abutting to the sea, many acres of boulders or stones which the washing of the tide has removed. The facing of the shore at this spot resembled that at Walmer Castle. Some early writers have supposed Cæsar's Naval Camp to have been in these sandhills, that is the old Haven midway between Deal and Sandwich, and that the sand mounds were called the work of the Romans. That these mounds have been brought together by the force of the wind is very improbable. From whence could the hillocks come? Surely not from the sea, nor from the long range of marsh land running on to Minster, nor from the high ground of Upper Deal and Northbourne, as all this land in all likelihood was covered with trees. The practice of raising mounds of earth over the remains of the dead was the custom of a very early period. Homer illustrates it by saying, as translated by Pope:

> "'Stern as he was—he yet revered the dead;
> Preserved his radiant arms from hostile spoil,
> And laid him decent on the funeral pile,
> Then raised a mountain where his bones were burned—
> The mountain nymphs his rural tomb adorned.'

"Some forty years ago, a labouring man, in digging for sand, discovered two Roman vases containing a great quantity of coin—a circumstance leading to the conclusion that the Romans buried their dead in these hills when they had full possession of the Island and were located at Richborough, the supposed place of residence of the Roman government of Britain for four centuries."

Whether or not these sandhills formed any part of Julius Cæsar's naval camp, there certainly were, and still are, remains of *other* entrenchments in Deal and Walmer which tradition points out to have been his work, and which have all the appearance of having been thrown up for such a purpose. It must be remembered that Cæsar constructed *two* naval camps at his place of landing, one during his first expedition, and the other, a much larger one, on his second invasion of the country, and that on each occasion his ships were shattered by a tempest; so that it may well have happened that some were driven in the direction of these sandhills, and were there repaired by being first drawn into dykes or basins dug out in the sand, where they would be protected from the violence of any future tempest that might arise.

With regard to the remarkable entrenchments in Deal itself, Leland in his Itinerary, published in the reign of Henry VIII., gives the following account:—"Deale, half a myle fro the shore of the sea—a Finssheher villiage, three myles or more above Sandwic, is upon a flat shore, and very open to the se, wher is a fosse or a great bank, artificial, betwixt the town and se, and beginneth about Deale, and runneth a great way up towards the Clyse, in as much that sum suppose that this is the place wher Cæsar landed. Surely the fosse was made to keep owt ennemyes ther or to defend the rage of the se or by the casting up beche and pible."

Mr Pritchard remarks as follows concerning this fosse, thus described by Leland, and the ancient town of Deal:—"It is supposed by some writers that Upper and Middle Deal was the town described, particularly as Leland calls "Deale" a village, which meant in those early times houses and buildings standing together without being enclosed or protected by a wall surrounding it—as we can see the remains of such defences at Dover and Sandwich. The valley of Deal, now named Lower Street, was in that state so as to abut the sea in 1600. The singularity of this trench between Beach Street and West Street has caused considerable enquiries. The fosse or ditch described by the historian Leland, leads to the conclusion that it is artificial, thrown up as a fortification to defend the inhabitants from any attack by enemies on landing on the shore. This trench commences at the south end of the town, terminating at the north end by Peter Street. Our ancestors in building the New Town of Lower Deal never contemplated the time coming of its extension to the degree it has now attained. Had that been done when the trade and commerce increased in the time of Elizabeth, which led to the settlement of sea-faring people on its sea margin, the facility of drainage would have been the first consideration, and provision made for it; but as it is now, it must so remain, for to fill the valley up for the purpose of drainage would destroy the best part of the town."

This account, written in 1864, proves that the vestiges of Cæsar's entrenchments at Deal were then easily traceable; nor are there wanting at Walmer even now remains of earthworks which may have formed part of his naval camp, or advanced outposts in connection with it, for "round Walmer Church," says Mr Pritchard, "which stands at the south end of the village, on a rise is a deep fosse, and there are other visible signs of entrenchments at Hawkeshill Close, near the Castle to the southward, and on the place called Dane Pitts, on the old down not far distant." And, indeed, the very name of the place "Walmer," anciently called "Wall mare," "quasi vallum maris," as an old writer explains it, sufficiently indicates the existence formerly of an extensive fortification or sea-wall. Nor must we omit to mention that between the two downs or hill sides at Kingsdowne, near Walmer, were the remains of an ancient camp, of which place Darell says, that it was in our earliest history called "Roman Codde," and by the common people "Romny Coddy," which he explains to mean "the fortitude of the Romans." This place is too far distant to have formed part of Cæsar's naval camp, but it may have been an ancient British stronghold taken by the Romans in their incursions from the camp, and so associated with their name.

Such, then, are the indications, traditional and otherwise, which point to Cæsar's landing at Deal. And it must be observed that for centuries no question was ever raised as to any other place having a claim to that distinction. Whatever theories *modern* authors may have adopted with regard to his landing, and however vigorously they may have contended on behalf of other places, no *tradition* points to any other locality than Deal as the landing place of Julius Cæsar.

In saying this, we are not forgetful that several other places may boast of having been called "Cæsar's camp." Batteley speaks of a "Cæsar's camp" at Richborough, and a hill near Folkestone is still called by that name. There is also a "Cæsar's camp" near Findon in Sussex. But with regard to these places which lay claim to this title, it must be remembered that the mere name is handed down, and that no well-authenticated tradition points them out as having been the encampments of *Julius* Cæsar. That they may have been the camps of Cæsar, either of Claudius Cæsar or of Aulus Plautius, his general, and called by him after the emperor, or of Vespasian or Severus, may be readily conceded. In fact it is not improbable that the three camps at Richborough, Folkestone, and Findon, were thrown up by Aulus Plautius, who, as Dion Cassius narrates, "divided his forces into three portions, lest all arriving at one place he might be prevented from landing." What is more likely than that he chose for disembarking his army[1] the three most celebrated ports

[1] Aulus Plautius was sent over by Claudius with a double-consular army of 52,000 men, at the instigation of Bericus (or Vericus), a British chief who had been dispossessed of his territory. His landing was unopposed, the Britons being engaged in intestine wars, and unable to combine (as Bericus had informed Claudius) for the defence of their country. Geoffrey of Monmouth and Matthew of Westminster make him to have landed at Caer-Peris (Portchester), but their whole story of the event seems fabulous. From the account of his voyage by Dion Cassius, Plautius would appear to have sailed, perhaps with the main division of his army, in a westerly direction, and we find him defeating the Dobuni (the inhabitants of Gloucestershire), but whether he landed at Portchester or (as "Cæsar's camp," near Findon, would suggest) at Adurni is uncertain. It seems likely, however, that Plautius, having so large an army at his command, that he could divide it, would detach some portion to occupy the Kentish shore, where the Romans under Julius Cæsar had previously established themselves, and with this intent where could he

adjacent to these places, namely the Portus Rutupinus, Lemanis, and Adurni, the nearest ports (with the exception of Dover, which Julius Cæsar had found to be unsuitable for landing) to the coast of Gaul. Positions taken up by Aulus Plautius in the name of the Emperor Claudius would be more likely to be called "Cæsar's camps" than those associated with the expeditions of Julius Cæsar, for the Romans accorded the conquest of Britain to Claudius Cæsar rather than to the great founder of that

have landed better than at Rutupium (Richborough), and Lemanis (Lymne)? Although we read of no conquests made by him in Kent, Suetonius seems to account for this when he says that "a part of the island surrendered without the hazard of a battle or the shedding of blood." That Aulus Plautius occupied Kent is rendered probable by the statement of Dion Cassius, that Claudius, when summoned by his general, crossed over to Britain, and *at once* marched to *the Thames*. This he could not have done with such confidence had he not known that Plautius had previously occupied the country through which he would pass.

With regard to Bericus, the author would mention, as a coincidence of name, but without founding any argument upon it, that there is in the parish of Bridge, near Canterbury, a place formerly called Bereacre, now Great and Little Baraker, and that the very ancient road leading to it is known locally as "Bericus's road."

family. "Claudius," says Seneca, "might first glory in conquering the Britains, for Julius Cæsar no more than showed them to the Romans," and other Roman writers have used similar language, some even asserting that Julius Cæsar turned his back upon the Britons. With regard to the expedition of Aulus Plautius, it is certain that it was carried out in the emperor's name, for he had strict injunctions when any difficulty arose to send for Claudius. He of course took care that at the right opportunity the emperor should be summoned, and by this preconcerted plan the honour of the conquest was transferred from the general to the emperor himself, who was accorded a magnificent triumph on his return to Rome, and received the appellation of Britannicus. Is it not therefore extremely probable that Aulus Plautius, knowing his master's ambition, and perhaps having received instructions from him to do so, called each of the three camps which he fortified after landing his troops, as if pitched in the emperor's name, "Cæsar's camp"? However this may be, or whatever Roman emperor may have given them their name, it is certain that they could not *all* be the camps of Julius Cæsar, since his naval camp was on each occasion thrown up at the same place, nor did he form any other encampments near the sea. Since, however, Richborough, Lemanis, and Adurni present rival claims, we will leave to those who advocate them the task of deciding which are the strongest. For our own part we unhesitatingly assert on the authority of Cæsar's own narrative, interpreted by the only tradition extant, that the landing of Julius Cæsar was on the "open and level shore" of Deal, and that his naval camp extended along that shore as far as Walmer Castle.

CHAPTER IV.

CÆSAR'S FIRST EXPEDITION. EARLY ENCOUNTERS WITH THE BRITONS.

THE events connected with the landing of Cæsar on the shores of Britain, the gallant resistance he met with, the heroism and success of his soldiers, and the subsequent disasters which led him to leave the island for a time, form one of the most interesting and stirring pages of history.

When Cæsar loosed his vessels from their anchorage at Dover, the Britons, perceiving his design to land further along the coast, having sent forward cavalry and chariots, followed closely with their remaining forces, and endeavoured to prevent his disembarkation. From the lofty cliffs between Dover and Deal the scouts of their army could no doubt watch the progress of his vessels, while the main body of the Britons came by a shorter and easier route along the inland valley. That they were able to reach Deal in time to oppose his landing affords striking testimony not only to the rapidity of their movements, but to the excellence of the roads over which they travelled.

It must, however, be borne in mind that Cæsar, being imperfectly acquainted with the coast and the tides, chose an unfavourable time for the attempt to land his vessels, and so gave longer time for rallying to the enemy. According to the computation of Dr Halley, Leverrier, and others, he left Dover on the afternoon of the 25th of August B.C. 55, A.U.C. 699, on which day the moon would be at the full and the tide at its highest, and spring tides at about eleven o'clock in the forenoon. Consequently as he probably reached the shore at Deal about an hour after he set sail from Dover, that is at about four o'clock P.M., only two hours remained before it was low water, and, as his ships probably drew eight or ten feet of water, he would not be able at the ebb, and during spring tides, to bring them nearer than 1000 feet to the shore. "There was great difficulty," he says, "because the vessels on account of their size could not be stationed except in deep water. But the soldiers, oppressed with the great weight of their arms, ignorant of the ground, and with their hands encumbered, were obliged to leap from the ships, and to engage the enemy standing close in the waves;—while they on the other hand, either from dry land or having advanced a very little into the water, with all their limbs perfectly free, were boldly hurling darts from places with which they were well acquainted, and urging on horses inured to the service. Cæsar finding his men dismayed and disorganized by this unaccustomed manner of fighting, ordered his long-boats or galleys to be rowed a little distance from the transports, so as to attack the open flank of the enemy, and to dislodge them from their position by slings and arrows and other missiles. This manœuvre was of great service, for the Britons

CÆSAR'S FIRST EXPEDITION.   131

confused by the shape of the vessels, the motion of the oars, and the unusual kind of engines of war, stopped and drew back, though but for a little space. Still the Roman soldiers hesitated to leave their galleys on account of the depth of the water, and the temporary advantage gained might have been thrown away but for the bravery of the standard-bearer of the Tenth Legion, who calling upon the gods for the success of his venture, said with a loud voice, 'Leap down, soldiers, unless you wish to betray the eagle to the enemy; I at any rate shall have performed my duty to the State and my general.' With these words he threw himself from the vessel and began to bear the eagle towards the enemy. Then the rest of the soldiers encouraging one another, and fearing the disgrace of the loss of a Roman eagle, leaped down in a body from the vessel; and others from the nearest vessels, incited by their example, having closely followed, they approached the enemy.

"On both sides the battle was sharply contested. The Roman soldiers, unable to keep their ranks, or to stand firmly, or to follow closely their standards, fell into great confusion, while the Britons, knowing the shallows, whenever they beheld from the shore any of the enemy disembarking from their vessels, attacked them, encumbered as they were, from their chariots driven at full speed into the water, many thus surrounding a few, while others hurled darts from the open flank on the main body of the enemy.

"On seeing this, Cæsar ordered the boats belonging to the galleys, and the spy-boats, to be filled with soldiers, and sent them to help those whom he saw distressed. By thus bringing into action all his reserve forces, he at length revived the drooping courage of his legions, and the Romans having gained the shore, and their discipline being restored, they made a simultaneous attack upon the Britons and put them to flight. They could not, however, pursue them very far, owing to the vessels with the cavalry having been unable to gain the island through contrary winds. In this one particular his usual good fortune had failed Cæsar."

Such is the account given in "the Commentaries" of this memorable engagement, in which were so conspicuously displayed the bravery of the contending forces, and the skill and watchfulness of the great general who directed the attack. An incident of remarkable heroism is recorded by Valerius Maximus[1] as having occurred during the battle, which it is important to notice, as it affords corroborative evidence that the shore at Deal was the scene of the encounter. The account, as translated by Napoleon, is as follows:—"A certain legionary. Cæsius Scæva, having thrown himself into a boat with four men, reached a rock, whence with his comrades he threw missiles against the enemy; but the ebb rendered the space between the rock and the land fordable. The barbarians then rushed to them in a crowd. His companions took refuge in their boat; he, firm to his post, made an heroic defence, and killed several of his enemies; at last, having his thigh transpierced with an arrow, his face bruised by the blow of a stone, his helmet broken to pieces, his buckler covered with holes, he trusted him-

[1] "Val. Max." III., ii. 23.

self to the mercy of the waves, and swam back towards his companions. When he saw his general, instead of boasting of his conduct, he sought his pardon for returning without his buckler. It was, in fact, a disgrace among the ancients to lose that defensive arm; but Cæsar loaded him with praise, and rewarded him with the grade of a centurion." The same exploit is recorded by Eutropius from some pieces of Suetonius now lost. Camden gives the following translation of the passage:—"Scæva, one of Cæsar's soldiers, and four more with him, came over before in a little ship to a rock near the island, and were there left by the tide. The Britons in great numbers fell upon these few Romans; yet the rest of his companions got back again. Still Scæva continues undaunted, overcharged with weapons on all sides; first resisting them with his spear, and after with his sword, fighting there single against a multitude. And when he was at length both wearied and wounded, and had had his helmet and buckler beat out of his hand, he swam off with two coats of mail to Cæsar's camp; where he begged pardon for his rashness, and was made a centurion."

These accounts of Scæva's exploit bear a general similarity to one mentioned by Plutarch, and the name of the soldier is attributed by him to the hero of another deed of daring at Dyrrachium. In describing the valour and affection of Cæsar's soldiers for their general, Plutarch gives the following narrative:—" Cassius Scæva also, in a conflict before the city of Dyrrachium, having one of his eyes put out with an arrow, his shoulder stricken through with a dart, and his thigh with another, and having received thirty arrows upon his shield, he called to his enemies, and made as though he would yield to them. But when two of them came running to him, he clave the shoulder of one of them from his body with his sword, and hurt the other in the face, so that he made him turn his back, and at length saved himself, by means of his companions that came to help him. And in Britain also, when the captains of the bands were driven into a marsh or bog full of mire and dirt, and the enemies did fiercely assail them there, Cæsar then standing to view the battle, he saw a private soldier of his thrust in among the captains, and fight so valiantly in their defence, that at length he drove the barbarous people to fly, and by this means saved the captains, who otherwise were in great danger of being cast away. Then this soldier being the hindmost man of all the captains, marching with great pain through the mire and dirt, half swimming and half on foot, in the end got to the other side, but left his shield behind him. Cæsar, wondering at his noble courage, ran to him with joy to embrace him. But the poor soldier, hanging down his head, fell at Cæsar's feet, and besought him to pardon him, for that he had left his target behind him."

Now it is evident from the foregoing accounts that the story of Scæva's exploit was related with considerable variety of circumstance; in fact it would appear from Plutarch's account that Scæva was not the name of the hero of the brave deed in Britain, but of a somewhat similar adventure at Dyrrachium. There were, no doubt, many deeds of daring related of the soldiers in Cæsar's army, fireside stories passed from mouth to mouth. As is usual with such accounts, the details of the different stories became confused, the name of the hero of one being associated with another, each story growing in marvel as it travelled, until it was difficult to distinguish the substratum of truth upon which the narrative was founded. The story, however, as recorded by the three historians seems to be generally the same, namely, that one of Cæsar's soldiers, after a desperate encounter single-handed with several of the enemy on a rock near Cæsar's landing-place, at last escaped with many wounds and the loss of his target, for which he asked Cæsar's pardon and was made a centurion. The rocks mentioned by Valerius Maximus and Suetonius as the scene of this encounter may still be seen at low water during spring tides at Deal. They are known as "the Malms," and are opposite the naval yard and marine barracks. "There are other rocks," says Mr Pritchard, "at a greater distance from the shore, which the boatmen in running ashore can feel with their oars when the tide ebbs to a great extent. It is no uncommon thing for coins and valuable articles to be picked up from off these rocks, and the rocks must have existed for many years past just as they now are." It may be added that there are *no such rocks* at any of those other localities which have been named as the scene of Cæsar's disembarkation.

The decisive battle by which Cæsar effected the landing of his troops was succeeded by a temporary peace. Ambassadors were sent to Cæsar by the conquered Britons, promising their submission, and that hostages should be sent, in assurance of their future good behaviour. With these came Comius, the Atrebatian, whom Cæsar had sent before him into Britain. In waging war with the Britons Cæsar relied as much on intrigue and bribery as he did on skill and the bravery of his troops. The Atrebates, a Belgic people, having been conquered, Cæsar made Comius a regulus or petty king over them, and knowing his influence with the Atrebatian colony in Britain, and with the Britons generally, he sent him thither before he invaded the country, in order that he might win over to his cause whatever states he could. Comius doubtless met with some success in these endeavours, and it was probably through his means that negotiations were opened with Androgeus or Avarwy, whose treachery, as will be seen in the next chapter, was the cause of so much disaster to the Britons in Cæsar's second invasion of the country. The British historians indeed relate that Avarwy made a secret treaty with Cæsar prior to his first expedition, and that he was preparing to betray his country, and to throw open the gates of Caer Troia (London) to the conqueror, when the disaster which happened to his vessels compelled Cæsar to leave the country. Whatever success, however, Comius may have had at first in treating with some of the British chiefs, it was thwarted by the action of the people, who rose in indignation at the proposal of vassalage, and having seized Comius, threw him into prison. After the victorious landing of the Roman army, Comius was, as we have seen, restored to Cæsar, who, on the ground of this popular tumult which the British princes said they could not control, excused the treatment he had received, and contented himself with demanding a large number of hostages, of which some were surrendered at once, and others promised from more distant parts.

The peace thus concluded was destined to be of short duration. The fourth day after Cæsar's arrival in Britain a change of wind took place, which enabled the eighteen transport vessels with the cavalry to leave the port (Ambleteuse), and they were at length within sight of the naval camp (at Deal), when the shifting wind was succeeded by so violent a tempest that not one of them could hold its course. Some were driven back to the place whence they sailed, others to the coast of Cornwall, whence, after securing for a time safe anchorage, they eventually sailed back to the Continent.

The tempest, however, occasioned more serious disaster to Cæsar than the disappointment at not receiving his cavalry. His vessels lying at anchor near the shore were many of them completely wrecked, and even his galleys which were beached, the moon being at the full and the tide consequently very high, were filled with water, so that, having made no provision for a winter campaign, and having no means at his command for repairing his vessels, he was reduced for a time to a state of complete helplessness.

Seeing the desperate condition of the Romans, and judging them to be few in number from the smallness of their camp (for Cæsar, having no heavy baggage with him, had confined his encampment within narrow limits), the princes who had just made peace with Cæsar, having conferred together, decided to renew the war. They thought that by protracting it into the winter, and preventing all supply of provisions to the Romans, they would so subdue them that no foreign foe would hereafter venture to invade their country. Having therefore laid their plans they left the camp one by one, and withdrew their men from the fields.

Cæsar, although as yet he had no knowledge of their intention, nevertheless from their ceasing to bring hostages, suspected they were plotting some mischief. He at once prepared for every emergency. He brought in each day the corn from the fields, and by using the material of those vessels which were completely shattered, was able so to repair the others which had sustained less damage, that, twelve being broken up, the rest were rendered seaworthy.

Meanwhile the Britons were not slow in carrying out their design. Having reaped the corn everywhere except in one locality, they laid an ambush by night in the woods adjacent to this, so that when the seventh legion of the Roman army came there to forage, they rushed out upon them unawares, and having slain some, threw the rest into confusion by surrounding them with cavalry and chariots. The dust caused by these movements having attracted the notice of the guards on station before the camp, they reported the matter to Cæsar. He, taking with him the cohorts that were in advanced positions before the camp, at once went to the relief of his men. His arrival both revived the courage of his own soldiers, and arrested the onslaught of the enemy. Cæsar, however, does not claim to have won a victory. He held his ground, but deemed it inexpedient to provoke the enemy to a battle. Both armies retired from the contest, the Britons being so far victorious that they were suffered to carry away as prisoners those whom they had seized upon in the fields.

Such is the account given by Cæsar himself of this remarkable conflict, which drew from him unqualified admiration, not only of the chariot system in use among the Britons, but also of the dexterity and fearlessness with which they manœuvred. His description, which will be given in another chapter, brings vividly before us the heroic age and the chariot system of Troy as celebrated in the verse of Homer.

The British accounts of this engagement change *the drawn battle* of Cæsar's commentaries into a signal defeat sustained by the Roman legions. They are thus summarised by Mr Morgan. "The seventh legion was in the act of giving way, when Cæsar's arrival changed for a time the aspect of the engagement. But the repulse was of short duration. The British cavalry, under Nennius, attacked the tenth legion commanded by Cæsar in person; their infantry at the same time bore down and completed the success of the charge. The utmost efforts of the Roman general failed to remedy the confusion which ensued. In vain he threw himself into the melée. The disorder and mingling of the troops was irretrievable. His voice was lost in the tumult and din of the field. The eagle itself was borne down, and Cæsar in covering it with his body was assailed by Nennius. The sword of the great Roman buried itself in the shield of the British prince, and before he could extricate it, the tide of battle separated the combatants, leaving the weapon a trophy to be long afterwards exhibited to the inhabitants of Caer Troia. Cæsar performed all that an able general or intrepid soldier could do to recover the honour of the day. But fortune and superior skill were both against him. All that he could succeed in effecting was to prevent the British army entering the camp with the routed remains of his own legions."

In endeavouring to assign the locality of this engagement there are certain particulars mentioned in Cæsar's history which will assist us. First, the battle was fought out of view of the camp, the dust only caused by the strife being visible from the gates. Secondly, it was fought upon arable land, with woods close by, in which the Britons lay in ambush. Thirdly, there were stations of the Roman army in the direction of the battle-field, from which Cæsar drew his troops when advancing to the relief of his seventh legion. Taking these facts into consideration, it seems probable that the battle was fought in the neighbourhood of Ringwould and Martin Mill. It will be remembered that the British forces which opposed Cæsar's landing had *come from Dover*. They do not seem to have been drawn from distant parts, but were for the most part *local* forces. When defeated they would therefore naturally retire in the direction whence they came, so as, if necessary, to fall back upon their former strong position at Dover. Thus Ringwould and the neighbourhood of Martin Hill would lie on their direct line of retreat. This position moreover accords well with the details of the history. For in the first place, it is so situated that the rising ground between it and the shore would prevent the actual combat being seen from the camp, but

K

yet it is not so far distant, but that the dust raised by the manœuvres of the chariots and cavalry would be easily noticed by the guards before the camp. Secondly, the country inland from Deal was described by Cæsar as a plain and open shore, and to the present day is singularly barren of trees, while on the other hand the arable land between Ringwould and Martin Mill is skirted by the considerable woodlands of Oxney, which divide it from the shore. In these are the remains to all appearance of an ancient British Oppidum and chariot road, and the land bears every indication of having been covered with trees from a remote period. Thirdly, as mentioned by Mr Pritchard in his history of Deal, there were in his time at Kingsdown, between Cæsar's camp and Ringwould, the traces of a Roman encampment which bore locally the name "Roman Codde" (the fortitude of the Romans). Cæsar would be very likely to form an advanced post at this spot, for the little valley at Kingsdown, forming a break in the line of cliffs, would otherwise present a favourable opportunity for the Britons to approach by the seashore and attack his naval camp in rear or flank. The Commentaries, indeed, seem to indicate that there was a considerable encampment in the direction in which this engagement was fought, as a protection to the naval camp. The narrative states that Cæsar drew his relieving force from "the stations before the camp," and that he ordered these to be occupied by two other cohorts, that is by 1000 men (each cohort[1] consisting of about 500 men), and left word that others should follow. Cæsar then drew his troops from these advanced posts, as being doubtless in the direction in which he was advancing to succour his seventh legion; and in order that he might have a strong reserved force in case he should be defeated, he left word that two other cohorts, with others to follow, should occupy the vacated stations. In thus moving his troops along the shore, from his naval camp to the advanced camp at Kings-

[1] A legion consisted of from 5000 to 6000 men. Cæsar's legions probably contained about 5000. Ten cohorts constituted a legion. Each cohort therefore consisted of *about* 500 men, though the complement of soldiers was larger in some cohorts than in others.

down, he would have this advantage, that his supplies would be protected from the observation of the enemy by the line of cliffs between Walmer and Kingsdown.

In confirmation of the site we have named being the scene of the attack by the Britons on the foraging troops of the Romans, and the slaughter of many of them, it may be mentioned that in the construction of the Deal and Dover Railway a number of Roman urns, Samian and other ware, have been recently discovered near Martin Mill, some of which are in the possession of the owner of the adjoining property, Mr William Banks of Oxney Court. Many of these certainly belong to a subsequent period to that of Julius Cæsar, but it would only be in accordance with a general custom if the ground consecrated by the burial of these early Roman heroes who fell in the first invasion of the country, was afterwards used as a Roman cemetery.

The subsequent events connected with Cæsar's first expedition may be briefly narrated. "For many days in succession," he tells us, "tempestuous weather prevented both armies from resuming hostilities. This, at least, may be regarded as Cæsar's excuse for his own inactivity. The Britons, however, were not idle. Thinking to drive the comparatively small force of the invaders from their camp, and so for ever to free themselves from them, they despatched messengers in all directions, and having collected a large multitude both of infantry and cavalry, they advanced towards the camp. The issue of the battle that followed was such as might be expected, when an army gathered hastily from all parts attacked a well-disciplined force defended by a fortified position. Cæsar's legions were drawn up in array before his camp, and their rear being thus secured from attack, they fought with such confidence and intrepidity, that the Britons speedily gave way. They were pursued to some distance by the Roman soldiers, and Cæsar being now in possession of some thirty horse which Comius, the Atrebatian, had brought over to Britain with him, the rout was complete. The brave but over-matched defenders of their country were many of them slain, and their rude habitations destroyed. Their chiefs were fain to secure peace by promising twice the number of hostages that Cæsar had before required.

The great Roman general, although in the end victorious, had little cause to congratulate himself upon the results of his expedition. With a shattered fleet, and an army largely reduced in numbers, he was compelled to return to the continent, not having gained sufficient footing in the country to maintain his position through the coming winter. Such a conquest seemed hardly distinguishable from a defeat, and although a thanksgiving of twenty days was decreed by the Senate in his honour, there were not wanting those who declared his expedition a failure and a disgrace, and charged him openly with turning his back upon the victorious Britons.

CHAPTER V.

CÆSAR'S SECOND INVASION OF BRITAIN. HIS VOYAGE, INLAND MARCH, AND FIRST BATTLE.

THE account of Cæsar's second invasion of Britain commences with the eighth chapter of the fifth book of his Commentaries. He proceeds to relate that having left Labienus on the Continent with three legions and 2000 horse, for the protection of the ports and for the provisioning of corn, as well as to watch the course of events and act as occasion might require, he himself with five legions and 2000 horse, set sail at sunset with a gentle south-west wind.[1] The wind, however, having slackened about midnight, he did

[1] Napoleon has proved by calculations based upon various data that Cæsar started on his second expedition on July 21st, in the year A.U.C. 700, or B.C. 54.

not hold his course, but was carried too far by the tide, and at daybreak found that he had left Britain on his left hand. The tide changing, he endeavoured to gain by rowing that part of the island where he had found the previous summer a landing could be best effected. In this he was much assisted by the praiseworthy endurance of his soldiers in the transports and heavy boats, who by their unremitted exertions in rowing kept pace with the long and lighter vessels. Thus Britain was approached by all the vessels about mid-day. No enemy, however, was seen at the place of landing. Cæsar states, that he subsequently learned from the prisoners that great bands of the Britons had assembled there, but that being terrified by the number of his vessels (which with those built the previous year and the privateers amounted to more than 800), they had withdrawn to the higher grounds.

The reason Cæsar here gives for his landing being unopposed hardly accords with the brave and fearless character which the Britons had exhibited at his previous invasion of their country. A more probable reason, about which Cæsar himself is naturally silent, is furnished by the

Welsh, or rather British, history of the transaction. According to this account, Cæsar, prior to his first invasion of Britain, had, through the medium of Comius, opened secret communications with Avarwy or Androgeus, son of the last sovereign, Lud, and regarded by a powerful faction as the rightful heir to the throne.[1] A secret treaty

[1] This traitor has been identified with Mandubratius, a British chieftain, mentioned by Cæsar as having formed an alliance with him. The unpopularity of Avarwy with the great mass of the people was marked by the stigmatic name, "Du-bradwr" or "Mandubrad" (the Black Traitor). There are, however, some differences between the Cambrian account of Avarwy and Cæsar's account of Mandubratius. According to the former, Avarwy was the son of the last sovereign, Lud. Caswallon, after his election to the Pendragonate or military dictatorship of the whole island, treated Avarwy as his own son, giving him Kent and the whole territory between the Thames and the Wash for his princedom, and appointing him also governor of London. To his brother, Tenuantius, he also assigned the dukedom of Cornwall. Cæsar, on the other hand, says of Mandubratius, whom he calls the youth Mandubratius, that he was the son of Imanuentius, who had obtained the rule over the country of the Trinobantes (the district now comprising Middlesex and Essex), and had been killed by Cassivellaunus. Mandubratius himself escaped death by flight. Mandubratius, according to Cæsar, came to him in Gaul, and it would appear accompanied him to Britain in his second expedition, for we find from the subsequent history that, after Cæsar had defeated Cassivellaunus at the Thames,

was formed between them, by which, in return for Cæsar's support, Avarwy engaged, on the deposition of Caswallon (Cassivellaunus), to hold the kingdom as a tributary of Rome. The ill success of Cæsar's first expedition pre-

and had crossed that river, the Trinobantes sent ambassadors begging his protection for Mandubratius from the injustice of Cassivellaunus, and that he would send him to rule over them. The two accounts are not altogether irreconcilable. Each describes the person spoken of as a youth, and the son of a former sovereign; the one stating that his father's name was "Imanuentius," the other mentioning that his brother bore the very similar name, "Tenuantius." If Avarwy in the one account is identical with Mandubratius in the other, it is probable that the southern portion of the territory originally assigned to him by Cassivellaunus had been taken from him through distrust of his loyalty, and that, smarting under this supposed injustice, he went over to Cæsar in Gaul, hoping to regain his authority by traitorously bringing over the great Roman conqueror to his assistance. We are led to this supposition by the Welsh account, which states that Avarwy had command only over the Coranidæ, or Coritani, who inhabited some of the midland counties, and by Cæsar's own statement that the Trinobantes requested him to restore Mandubratius to his former rule over themselves. Cæsar would naturally suppress the fact that Mandubratius had departed from him in Gaul in order to return and play the traitor in Britain, and that it was through his treachery that he was afterwards able to land his army and conquer the Britons.

vented Avarwy at that time from carrying out his contemplated treachery. When, however, tidings reached the British chieftains that Cæsar intended a second invasion of the country (to quote the words of Mr Morgan), "The Gorsedd or high council of the nation was convened by Caswallon in London. Avarwy and his faction attended in large numbers. The decision arrived at is known in the Triads as *the first of the three fatal counsels of the Isle of Britain*. Caswallon, who had already posted detachments of troops along the coast, urged the policy of opposing so formidable an invader, as before, on the beach itself, and thus preventing a single hostile camp being thrown up on British soil. Avarwy, on the contrary, maintained that it was derogatory to the honour of the nation to adopt any other plan of action than one which would at once bring the Romans and Britons face to face on an equal field with each other, that every facility for landing ought to be afforded Cæsar, that the great lesson to be taught the continent was, that Britain relied for the maintenance of her liberties, not on her inaccessibility as an island, but on the natural courage of her own children. The insidious advice prevailed. The council resolved "that it was beneath the dignity of the nations of the Britons to defend their country otherwise than by the might of manhood, and that the landing of the Cæsaridæ be unopposed."

The motives which actuated **Avarwy** in giving this fatal advice were not only that he might enable Cæsar to land his army, but that he might draw the British forces into a position at which he could with safety desert with his forces to the Romans. The sequel will show how he afterwards carried out this traitorous intention.

But let us proceed with Cæsar's narrative. "The army," he says, "being set on shore, and a proper place chosen for the camp, when Cæsar learnt from the captives in what place the forces of the enemy had pitched, having left ten cohorts and 300 horse by the sea as a guard to the vessels, he himself, at the third watch of the night, advanced towards the enemy, having little fear for his vessels, because he was leaving them at anchor on a smooth and open shore, and he appointed over the guard for the vessels Quintus

Atrius. After a night march of about twelve miles, he came in sight of the forces of the enemy." We may remark here that Cæsar, notwithstanding his own statement to the contrary, must have obtained very accurate information as to the movements of the British forces, to have ventured on a march of twelve miles by night in an enemy's country, and that too on the same night on which he landed. The hilly ground between Deal and Dover[1] would have afforded a favourable position from which an enemy encamped there might have attacked his rear; and had he not ascertained to a certainty that there were no British forces in the neighbourhood, it would have ill accorded with his usual prudence to have ventured with the greater part of his army so far from his base of operations, leaving only ten cohorts (equal to one legion) and 300 horse as a protection to his ships, and at the risk of having his retreat cut off. He tells us indeed that he learned the disposition of

[1] The traces of fortified positions may be found at Walmer near the old church, and at Oxney. As before stated, at the latter place, about midway between Deal and Dover there are the remains of what was evidently a well-fortified British oppidum.

the enemy's forces from the captives, and we know that Cæsar usually took with him in his marches the captives taken in previous engagements, and that he had taken many captives in his previous invasion of Britain. But these captives could not have informed him as to the enemy's present position; and a few stragglers captured, even if he found any (which is hardly likely) immediately upon landing on the beach at Deal, could not be relied on to give accurate information as to the movements of the British now more than twelve miles distant. On the contrary, Cæsar's *rapid movement shows that he had a preconcerted scheme,* an accurate knowledge of the enemy's plans, a definite understanding with some secret ally, such as we find from the British account he had with Avarwy.

It will be necessary to be more discursive in our comments upon Cæsar's history of his progress from this point, for one of the principal objects of these pages is to trace the course of his army during the *next two days,* as marked out by historical, local, and traditional knowledge. After his march of twelve miles from the coast he came in sight of the enemy, and he relates: "They having proceeded with chariots and cavalry to the river, began from the higher ground to check the advance of our men, and to join battle." The direction which Cæsar took on this occasion has been examined with great attention to detail by Napoleon III. From the measurements of his surveyors he has ascertained that a circle with a twelve mile radius, having Deal for its centre, touches the river Stour (*i.e.*, the river now known as the *lesser* Stour[1])

[1] Napoleon writes: "This stream is incontestably the *flumen* of 'the Commentaries.' There is less room for error, as we find no other stream in the part of the county of Kent comprised as between the coast of Deal and the Great Stour, and as this latter runs too far from Deal to answer to the text. Although the little Stour is not, between Barham and Kingston, more than from three to four metres broad, we need not be astonished at the denomination of *flumen* given to it by Cæsar, for he employs the same expression to designate simple rivulets such as the Ose and Oserain" (De Bello Gallico, vii. 69, Alesia). Napoleon also points out that it should not be expected from the recital of "the Commentaries" that the river was a very wide one, as "Cæsar's cavalry passed it without difficulty, and this fact forms an objection to the Great Stour which several authors, and amongst others General de Gœler, take for the *flumen* of the text; it is sufficiently broad and sufficiently steep-banked towards Sturry, where they place

along an arc, the two extreme points of which are at Kingston and Littlebourne. Napoleon inclines to the opinion that Kingston was the place where the two armies first joined battle, as answering best to the description in " the Commentaries ; " although he admits it to be doubtful whether that or Littlebourne was the first battlefield. From traces of encampments which still remain, there is every reason to believe that Cæsar's army advanced towards both these localities. In marching from the coast, especially the scene of the action to render the passage difficult for cavalry. Moreover Sturry is fifteen and not twelve miles from the coast of Deal."

There is, however, every reason to believe that the lesser Stour, though not so wide and deep in Cæsar's time as to prevent the passage of cavalry, was formerly a very much wider stream, and more worthy the designation of " flumen " than it is at the present day. Among the authorities who have written on this subject the following from the Rev. Bryan Faussett may be quoted :—" In the bottom, between the village of Kingston and these tumuli, (referring to numerous tumuli on Barham Downs,) there is what in this part of Kent is commonly called an Aylebourne, Naylebourne, or rivulet, which though it is not now-a-days a constant but occasional stream, yet certainly was in former ages by no means unworthy the name of a river. And such indeed it is at this day, at the small distance of but a mile lower, namely to the north-

during the night, Cæsar would not strike out into the open country, but would follow the course of the ancient British road, probably that which may still be traced, and which tradition refers to an early period, from the Strand at Deal passing

west where it still retains the name of the Lesser Stour, and where it is seldom or never dry, but continues its course through Bishopsbourne, Bridge, Patricksbourne, and Bekesbourne, till at last it joins the greater Stour. Up to which last mentioned place (viz., Bekesbourne) there was, in the time of Edward III. and long after, a small navigation out of the Greater Stour. And as a proof of this Aylebourne having been much deeper and broader than it ever now is, I myself saw the shells of mussels turned plentifully out of the ground in digging a hole for a post at the distance of at least ten rods from its present channel, and at the perpendicular height of no less than three feet above its usual level." It may be added that the Greater Stour must have also been much wider in the time of Cæsar than it is now. It emptied itself into the Wantsum, and was probably tidal as far as Canterbury. This is indicated by the geological aspect of the surrounding land, and it may be mentioned in confirmation that the skeleton of an ox in an upright position, as if submerged while standing in the river, was some years ago dug out of the meadows near Canterbury. It is certain then that Cæsar could not have crossed the Stour at Sturry (as Dr Guest and others contend that he did) without experiencing considerable difficulty, especially for his cavalry. This would be contrary to what his "Commentaries" imply was the case.

through Upper Deal, Knowlton, Goodneston, and Adisham. Proceeding with all his forces by this road as far probably as what is now known as Adisham Mill, a remarkably elevated situation, he descried the British forces, where indeed from the information of Avarwy he had expected to find them, lining the crest of the hill (described in "the Commentaries" as "superior locus") from Garrington (near Littlebourne) on his right hand, to probably the part of Barham Downs opposite Bridge and Bishopbourne on his left. This was the best position which the Britons could possibly have chosen for the purpose of arresting the progress of an army marching upon Caer Caint (Canterbury); for the hills there are higher than any others in the immediate neighbourhood, varying from 190 to 120 feet above the sea level, as shown by the depth of the wells. We may assume that Cæsar, in accordance with his usual tactics, deployed his forces, after descrying the enemy, in three divisions, so as the more readily to extend them in line of battle, the vanguard moving to the right towards Garrington, forming the right wing of his army, the centre advancing towards Bridge Hill, the rear guard extending to the left (as the left wing) to drive the enemy from their position on Barham Downs, where they threatened to intercept his approach to the river. This would be the probable disposition of the Roman forces, and we have reason to believe that they afterwards occupied and fortified these localities.

The first encounter seems to have been for the most part a cavalry engagement. This would naturally be the case. After a forced march of twelve miles through a country where he would meet with no streams of water, Cæsar's first thought would be to obtain water for his horses. The river being apparently open to him, or only weakly defended at Charlton (in Bishopsbourne), he directed his cavalry there in the first instance. The Britons, thinking that this was a movement to outflank them, rushed down, as Cæsar relates, "from the higher ground" with their chariots and their cavalry to the river;" no doubt to check their advance and prevent their reaching the stream. That the Britons were traditionally reported to have opposed

Cæsar's progress *before he reached* the river, rather than after passing it, may be inferred from the following passage from Pomponius Sabinus, out of Seneca: "And in the night marching twelve miles up into the country, Cæsar finds out the Britons, who *retreated as far as the river*, but gave him battle there."

The battle was a terrible one, but decisive. The Roman cavalry, of which there were 1700 (300 only out of the 2000 brought over by Cæsar having been left at the naval encampment at Deal), completely routed the enemy, and drove them into the woods. The right wing of Cæsar's army encountered no resistance, for at Garrington it is probable that Avarwy and his Coranidæ were stationed, and these at once deserted to the Romans. A gallant resistance, however, was offered by the Britons, who had sought refuge in the woods. "Being repulsed," says Cæsar, "by our cavalry, they withdrew themselves into the woods, and reached a place excellently fortified both by nature and art, which they had prepared before on account, as it seemed, of some domestic war, having closed all the approaches to it by felled timber. They, few in number,[1] defended it from the woods, and prevented our men from entering the fortifications. The soldiers of the seventh legion, however, having formed a tortoise, and thrown up a mound against the fortifications, took the place, and drove them from the woods, a few wounds having been received."

The woods here mentioned still to a considerable extent remain. Beyond them, along the brow of the hill looking towards Canterbury, is " the green spot," so called in the British narrative of the battle,—now known as Patrixbourne Hill. It has been a burial-place of many generations. British, Roman, Saxon, Danish warriors here doubtless lie side by side, each nation, in accordance with an universal custom in those early times,

---

[1] The words of Cæsar, "ipsi rari propugnabant ex silvis," might be translated, " They in small detached parties defended it from the woods;" but this rendering does not seem to agree with the statement that the Britons found protection in an oppidum, all the approaches to which had been *closed*. That the Romans found it necessary to throw up a mound against the rampart proves that the difficulty in taking it arose, not from the opposition of small parties outside, but from the strength of its defences, and from the obstinate resistance of its garrison.

regarding a place of sepulture once set apart as devoted for such uses in perpetuity. These places were generally on the highest ground of the neighbourhood, and near the public roads.[1] The ground of Patrixbourne Hill, except where roads have since intercepted it, has not been disturbed for many centuries. It is still "the green spot," the chalky subsoil presenting no inducement to the agriculturist to disturb it with the plough. Thus has nature preserved the site of the fight for liberty so gallantly made by our British forefathers. Through the woods and down the green slope of Patrixbourne Hill, the Britons overpowered by numbers fled, and were pursued, many being cut down in their flight. A brave few, however, for some time arrested the onslaught of the enemy. A British Thermopylæ was found in an ancient oppidum[2] prepared for purposes of de-

[1] Many very interesting specimens of ancient pottery, and glass, brazen, and other ornaments, as well as iron spear heads and swords, with human remains, were dug up some years ago on Patrixbourne Hill. They belonged to various periods. Some have been deposited in the Maidstone and Canterbury museums, and an interesting collection has been carefully preserved at Bifrons, the residence of the Marquis Conyngham.

[2] Cæsar (v. 21) says: "The Britains call that an oppidum

fence in their intestine wars. All the approaches to this oppidum were so protected by timber laid across and interlaced that the Roman cavalry could not dislodge the garrison which held it; and it was not until the soldiers of the seventh legion (Cæsar's favourite and most reliable corps) formed a tortoise with their shields, and under cover of it threw up a mound against the rampart, that they were able to scale its height. Even then its gallant defenders, though completely outnumbered, did not give way without inflicting some loss upon the enemy.

Now were we unable to discover any vestiges of this stronghold, there would be wanting one important link in the chain of evidence by which we identify the locality of Cæsar's first battleground. But the position of this oppidum can be readily assigned. Tradition points to a spot in Bourne Park not far from the road leading up Bridge Hill as the scene of the last struggle of these brave defenders of their country. It

where they have been used to assemble to avoid an incursion of enemies, when they have fortified the entangled woods with a rampart and a ditch."

bears the name of "Old England's Hole" or hollow, and has always been associated by local tradition with some gallant but ineffectual defence of the early inhabitants of the country against their invaders. "Never forget, my son," said the father of him whose researches and suggestions have done so much to inspire the writer of these pages, "never forget that this is 'Old England's Hole,' and that here a last stand was made for liberty by your British forefathers." An examination of "Old England's Hole" affords abundant confirmation of this tradition. Its situation is just where we might expect to find the oppidum mentioned in the history. "This place," says Napoleon, "must not be sought for far from the scene of the first encounter;" "England's Hole" is only a few hundred yards from the locality where we have placed that encounter, and from the outskirts of the woods into which, Cæsar says, the Britons retired. Its size is such that while it was a formidable stronghold, it might easily be defended by a few men. The rampart and ditch by which it was surrounded may still be traced. An agger or mound (probably that thrown up by the Roman soldiers, as it is evidently not part of the fortifications of the place, but thrown up as it were against them from without) still remains as if to prove the accuracy of Cæsar's narrative. Cross roads, traces of which may still be seen within fifty yards of the enclosure, afforded the garrison of the oppidum a ready means of escape if necessary. One especially, the ancient Roman Watling Street, but before that in all probability a British road, runs close to the enclosure, below the modern road by which Bridge Hill is now ascended. Numerous trees, giving it the appearance of an ancient grove, afford some indication of what its strength must have been when to trees, the progenitors of these, were fastened and interlaced the felled timber by which, as we read in "the Commentaries," it was rendered yet more impregnable. Nor are there wanting other proofs of a struggle having taken place at this spot. When the present road on Bridge Hill was dug out in 1829 five or six Roman urns,[1] with six or eight human

[1] These urns are thus alluded to in the report of the first meeting, at Canterbury, of the Archæological Association:

skulls, were discovered about five feet below the surface, embedded in the chalk. The remains also of a horse in a ferruginous condition were found within the oppidum by some boys about fifteen years ago.

The few brave defenders of this oppidum being at length dislodged, the victory of the Romans was fully assured and the rout complete. Circumstances, however, prevented Cæsar from following up his advantage to its full extent. "Cæsar," says the history, "forbade his men to follow the

" It is remarkable that the hill above Bourne (called, from the neighbouring village, Bridge Hill), where the Saxon barrows are found, appears to have been previously a Roman cemetery; for about twelve years ago, when the new Dover road was cut through it, a number of Romano-British urns and earthen vessels were discovered, with skeletons and fragments of weapons, at a greater depth than the Saxon graves. Some of these urns, now in the possession of Mr W. H. Rolfe of Sandwich, were exhibited by that intelligent antiquary at the meeting of the primeval section." The Rev. J. Hughes-Hallet, of Higham, also possesses one of the urns. In a tumulus about eighty feet from the oppidum, Lord A. Conyngham (so the author is informed by the workman who opened it for him) found, together with a human skull and bones, a breastplate of silver, a curved sword six inches out of line, two bronze shoulder-pieces, four spear-heads, and a wooden vessel banded with bronze bands.

fugitives too far, both because he was ignorant of the nature of the place, and because a great part of the day was now spent, and he wished time to be left for the fortification of the camp." Caesar had a general knowledge of the locality from information received from Avarwy, and from the captives he had brought over from Gaul, as well as from the numerous scouts which he employed whenever circumstances permitted. But the country into which his forces were now pursuing the enemy was densely wooded. At any point his soldiers might be taken in an ambush through ignorance of the positions of the various oppida (of which Caesar says there were many), and which were generally concealed from view by thick foliage. Partly for this reason, and partly because in accordance with the universal custom of the Roman armies, he wished to fortify his camp for the night, Caesar recalled his men.

This step, however, would in any case have been advisable in consequence of the great fatigue his soldiers had undergone. For two nights and nearly two days they had had no rest, and a recapitulation of the history will show that during this period, extraordinary exertions had been required of them. They had set sail from the Portus Itius at sunset, and the first night had been spent in anxiety upon an unknown sea, their vessels being carried out of their course by the tide. From daybreak of the next day until noon Cæsar's soldiers were arduously employed in rowing the transports and heavy boats in order to regain the ground they had lost, and to land at the desired point of the shore. The rest of the day had been occupied in disembarking and securing their vessels. Another night followed, in which they were allowed no rest, but marching for the distance of twelve miles, they halted at daydawn, only to prepare for an immediate and sharply fought contest, which, although the recital of it occupies only a brief space in Cæsar's "Commentaries," lasted, with the subsequent rout and pursuit, till the day was far spent. Such unusual labours, with the necessary duty still before them of fortifying their camp before they could retire for the night, must have rendered it absolutely necessary, were there no other reasons for it, that the troops should be recalled from the pursuit.

CHAPTER VI.

CÆSAR'S SECOND INVASION. HIS FIRST INLAND ENCAMPMENT.

N searching for the defences which Cæsar threw up after the victory recorded in the last chapter, and which were afterwards, during his absence at the place of disembarkation, more strongly fortified, we must not expect to find any traces of stone battlements or walls of brick. "It is certain," says the Rev. John Batteley, in his History of Rutupium, "that C. Julius Cæsar, both because of the continual movements of his troops in war, and because of the brevity of his stay in our island, left no camps except such as were hastily thrown up, and constructed only of turf and earth." Mr Batteley might have added

that from this very fact the vestiges of his camps may be expected to be the better preserved, mounds and fortifications of earth remaining clearly defined, especially in chalky soil, as the sepulchral tumuli in all parts of the world testify, for many centuries, long after buildings of stone and brick have entirely disappeared.

It has before been stated that the Roman forces were probably, on Cæsar's arrival at Adisham Mill or thereabout, extended in three divisions, the right wing towards Garrington, the centre towards Bridge Hill, and the left wing towards Charlton. That having occupied the positions at these localities, they afterwards fortified them, is evidenced by the remains of encampments and lines of earthworks still traceable at these places. Let us visit them in turn.

And first we bend our steps to what may be called "the heights of Garrington." Passing through the meadows at the back of Bekesbourne Vicarage we are struck by the unusual character of the hills to the right of us. Terrace rises above terrace, sometimes three, sometimes four or five, succeeding one another. Nature never

CÆSAR'S FIRST INLAND ENCAMPMENT. 175

formed them. We see here the defences found by experience to be the only effective ones against the formidable British chariots which struck such terror into the hearts of the Roman soldiers. It may be well to refer to Cæsar's description of the chariot mode of warfare as practised by the Britons. "This is the way of fighting from Chariots. First they drive about everywhere, and hurl darts; and generally cause disorder in the ranks by the very terror of the horses and the noise of the wheels, and when they have forced an entrance among the troops of horse, they leap down from the chariots and fight on foot. The charioteers meanwhile withdraw a little from the battle, and so dispose themselves that if those who are fighting should be pressed by a multitude of the enemy they may have a ready retreat to their own men. Thus they present in battle the mobility of horse, and the steadiness of foot soldiers, and they accomplish so much by daily use and exercise that on downhill and precipitous ground they are accustomed to hold up their horses when at full speed, and to manage and turn them in a short space, and to run along the pole, and to stand upon the yoke, and thence to get back into their chariots with very great rapidity."[1] The student of Homer will recognise in this description a remarkable similarity to the chariot system of ancient Troy, and

[1] The chariot here described by Cæsar was called "Essedum" (from the British "Ess," a carriage). It carried several warriors, who were by its means enabled to transport themselves to any part of the battle where they could engage the enemy with the greatest effect, the headlong career of the chariots meanwhile causing great disorder in the enemies' ranks. The charioteers were called "essedarii."

The *scythed* chariots, said to have been also in use among the Belgi and Britons (Mela., iii. 6; Lucan, i. 426; Silius, xvii. 422), were called "Covini" (from the British Cowain, a waggon), and the drivers, who appear to have been their sole occupants, "covinarii." They had hooks or scythes fastened to the axles and other parts of the chariots, and being driven furiously among the enemy, committed great havoc, mowing down all who could not escape from them. We find mention of them among some other nations. Thus the Nigritæ are reported by Frontinus and Strabo to have used them in their wars, and the Cyrenians, a neighbouring people, delivered over to Thimbro (in the time of Alexander) half of their armed chariots. Antiochus Eupator also invading Judæa, apparently with a Greek force (B.C. 163), brought with him 350 chariots. Hirtius also (Bell. Alex., lxxv.) states that scythed chariots were employed by Pharnaces against Cæsar with great effect:—"Our ranks being not yet formed, the scythed chariots disordered and confused the soldiers."

will be disposed to regard with some interest the claim of the Britons to be of Trojan descent.

Against this mode of warfare the only effective defence was an embankment so precipitous that the chariots could not surmount it, and accordingly all British strongholds were surrounded by these steep embankments very frequently, as at Garrington, one above another. Let us ascend the " heights of Garrington[1] along the course of the old chariot road (characteristic of all British oppida[2]) which leads up to the inner rampart.

---

[1] This name, according to Hasted, was formerly "Garwinton," and in the Domesday Survey was written "Warwinton." It is reasonable to suppose that it took its origin from its fortified and commanding position.

[2] It may be objected that this and other similar narrow roads were boundaries between different properties. It is very probable that they were so used, but judging from their breadth and depth they certainly could not have been originally framed for that purpose; nor can we in this way explain the remarkable fact that to all British oppida, wherever they are found, similar roads may almost invariably be traced. The reason why old roads and escarpments became the boundaries of estates is not difficult to assign. When petty chieftains or lairds established themselves by right of conquest or by settlement upon the soil, and others began to settle around them, it became necessary to define their estates,

Ascending by this winding road, which commences from the extreme left of the hill, we reach at last an open plateau, from which we can survey the country beneath us. Let any military man stand on this high ground and walk along its whole length overlooking the terraced battlements, and he will at once acknowledge it to be a very commanding position. To his right is a considerable extent of marshy ground, even at the present day, although drained off in ditches, sometimes flooded in winter. The lesser Stour, which winds its way through this marshy ground, was, as we have before remarked, at one time a much wider stream than it is now, and navigable by vessels as far as Bekesbourne. It is certain then that the land to the left of Garrington was at the time of Cæsar everywhere a morass, with a river flowing through it. An army stationed on these heights would therefore have no reason to fear an attack upon its right, and the lines of earth-

and they claimed such boundaries for their properties as they found to be already existing. Thus ancient roads and escarpments came in time to be planted with hedges or other landmarks, the better to preserve the limits of estates.

works, by which the position is so well protected, would render it practically impregnable in front.

But it may be urged, "This is no *Roman* camp; it has none of the straight and exact lines which the Romans generally laid down in measuring out their camps; it has more the appearance of a British stronghold." And so in fact it was,—a part of Cæsar's camp, but fortified, perhaps long before, but if not, at any rate at the time of his encampment on Barham Downs, after the British mode. A reference to the British histories will afford the explanation of this. It has already been mentioned that, during the battle on Barham Downs and at Old England's Hole, Avarwy with the Coranidæ under his command went over, according to a preconcerted plan, to the Romans. These deserters were probably, as we have stated, originally opposed in position to the right wing of the Roman army, and after their desertion formed part of that wing. It is certain at any rate that in a subsequent battle fought after Cæsar's return from his naval camp, their forces were opposed to the left wing of the British force, for we read in the British account of the battle, "On *the left*" (opposed therefore to the Roman right) "the battle raged between Nennius (a leader of the Britons) and the Coranidæ." The British position to the right of the marshy ground below Garrington is indicated by the description, also from a British source, "The British army occupied the open ground" (opposite the green slope), "its left wing under Nennius, *resting on a marsh*." On the Garrington heights, therefore, we may assume that the Coranidæ, of which there were 20,000 under Avarwy, encamped after their desertion to the Romans, overlooking on their right the marshy ground before described. Fearful as to the consequences of their treachery, they threw up, if not previously existing, these formidable battlements which no enemy could with impunity assail. Supported, no doubt, by a considerable Roman force, they were permitted, being so numerous a body, to fortify their camp after their own manner.

Leaving then Garrington, with its garrison of Coranidæ, let us next visit Cæsar's own camp on Barham Downs. That these downs were the scene of Cæsar's first inland battle and encampment tradition universally asserts, and we have the direct statement recorded on the chart found in Dover Castle, that "Cæsar having landed at Deal, afterwards conquered the Britons on Barham Down, a plain hard by, passable for horses, and fit to draw up an army in." A very superficial examination of the ground will show here the traces of Roman encampments. The two historians who have given descriptions of Roman castra are Polybius, who wrote about B.C. 140, and Hyginus, who wrote about A.D. 110. Plans of these two camps, the first of which was for two legions, and the second for three legions, are given in Dr Smith's "Dictionary of Antiquities." The two plans differ as to the dimensions and the internal divisions of the camps, but they have certain points in common which we should therefore expect to find in any Roman castra thrown up between these two dates. These common characteristics are first the rampart and ditch which formed the defence all round the camp, except at the four gates; secondly, the intervallum or intervening space (in the camp of Polybius 200 feet, and in that of Hyginus 60 feet) between the rampart and the camp itself; thirdly, the clearly defined roads marking out the different divisions of the camp, and which crossed one another at right angles. Examining the ground on Barham Downs with the view of tracing these characteristics, we are unable to describe with certainty the boundary ramparts enclosing the camp. From the extent of the ground apparently used for the purpose of encampment, there were probably two large oblong castra of the shape of that of Hyginus, the one extending along Barham Downs opposite Charlton, the other at the western extremity of the Downs extending over part of Bridge Hill, Bourne Park, and perhaps the grounds of Higham. Be this as it may, there can be no question that the remarkable parallel lines, in some places several exactly 60 feet apart, in others 20, 40, or 50 feet apart, with others intersecting at right angles, formed the dividing roads or vias of a Roman encampment. With the exception of these clearly marked lines excavated for military purposes, and the trenches dug out for the purpose of defining the race course which run in a different direction to the lines of the

Roman camp, it may be asserted with certainty that the Barham Downs have been undisturbed by man from time immemorial. They have always been used for pasturage only, the chalk with large flints interspersed on which the turf grows rendering them unsuitable for any other purpose; and there is no conceivable reason, except a military one, why these deep ditches or roads which are traceable on all parts of "the Downs" should have been dug out. When we consider that Cæsar's army with the camp followers could not have been less than 40,000 men, besides the 20,000 Coranidæ under Avarwy at Garrington, there can be no doubt that camps covering the whole ground which we have described would be required.

The question may arise whether the encampments traceable on Barham Downs were not the work of some of those armies which it is well known were encamped there in more recent times. It may be well, therefore, to note the various occasions when the Downs have been so occupied.

During the period of the Saxon and Danish

invasions we do not read of any resistance being offered in this immediate neighbourhood to their incursions, except perhaps on one occasion,[1] and

---

[1] The exception was the battle of Mercredesburne, which, as the site of it has not been before clearly identified, it will be well to describe. Several chroniclers of the Anglo-Saxon period have recorded this battle. The fullest account is that given by Henry of Huntingdon in his annals of the year A.D. 485. After describing the landing of Aella and his three sons Cymen, and Wlencing, and Cissa, he says, "The Britons fled as far as the nearest wood which is called Andredeslige. But the Saxons occupied the Sussex seashore more and more, seizing for themselves the land of the boundary until the ninth year of their coming. But then when they had seized too boldly the distant boundary, the kings and sovereigns of the Britons met at *Mercredesburne*, and fought against Aella and his sons, and the victory was almost doubtful: for each army being thoroughly injured and threatened, cursing the attack of the other, returned to their own. Aella therefore sent to his compatriots demanding help."

The same events are thus described in the Anglo-Saxon Chronicle:—A.D. 477. "This year Aella and his three sons, Cymen, and Wlencing, and Cissa, came to the land of Britain with three ships, at a place which is named Cymenesora, and there slew many Welsh, and some they drove in flight into the wood which is called Andredslea." A.D. 485. "This year Aella fought against the Welsh *near the bank of Mearcraedsburn.*"

Florence of Worcester also gives the following account :—
" A.D. 485. Aella in a battle with the Britons near *Mearcredes-*

the conflict did not then take place on Barham Downs, or indeed on that side of the river Stour. Canterbury was more than once ravaged by these

Burn, that is *Mearcred's Brook*, slew many of them, and put the rest to flight."

The battle lastly is thus described in the Chronicle of Fabius Ethelwerd:—" Aella arrived in Britain from Germany with his three sons at a place called Cymenes-ora, and pursued the Britons to a place called Aldredesleage. After eight years more the same chiefs attack the Britons near a place called *Mercredes-burnan-stede*."

Now, independently of any argument to be derived from the name of the site of this battle, as it is variously given by the different chroniclers, there is reason to believe that the country to the west of the lesser Stour must have been the scene of it. For the Saxon chronicle (see A.D. 893) states that the great wood of Andred extended from east to west 112 miles or longer, that it was 30 miles broad, and that the sea-port at the eastern end was Limene (Lymne). It is added that the river Limene (probably the Rother) *flowed out of the weald;* so that it is evident that the wood itself extended still further eastward, and there is therefore every reason to believe that the extensive woods called Atchester, Gorsley, and Whitehill, and other woods in the neighbourhood of Elham, Hardres, and Petham, were offshoots of the forest of Anderida or Andredeswold.

Now according to the quotation given above from Henry of Huntingdon, Aella, at his first landing, pursued the Britons into the wood of Andred, and then for eight years gradually encroached upon the land of the boundary along the sea coast, until at last venturing too boldly to seize the distant boundary,

devastating hordes, but their approach to the city was either from Rutupium or Lemanis, and after a weak resistance at those places their progress was practically unopposed, and was simply a continued

he was stoutly resisted by the British, and compelled to retire within his own lines. Now the meaning of the above account seems to be this: Aella, being unable to drive the British out of so immense a forest, contented himself with extending his conquests along the sea coast, until at last arriving at the termination of the wood, somewhere to the east of Lymne, he ventured inland, when he was opposed by the British at Mercraedsburn. This, as we have shown, would place the scene of the battle somewhere on the confines of the woods Atchester, Whitehill, Gorsley and others, which were the extreme eastward limits of the Forest of Anderida.

But there is other evidence that the scene of the battle was in this neighbourhood. The locality where it took place is variously described by the different chroniclers as " Mercredesburne," " near the bank of Mercraedsburn," " near Mearcredesburne, that is Mearcred's Brook," and " near a place called Mercredes-burnan-stede." Now, as there is no other brook outside the eastern limits of the wood of Andred except the Lesser Stour, which takes its rise in the Elham valley, this river must, I imagine, be the burn (or brook) here intended; and the termination of the name " Mercredsburn " seems to confirm this, since the Lesser Stour was formerly called " the Burn " (or " Bourne "), as we may surely gather from the fact that most of the villages through which it now passes, namely, Bishopsbourne, Patrixbourne, Bekesbourne, and Littlebourne, retain the suffix " burn " or " bourne " to the present

course of rapine and slaughter. Nor is there any reason to believe that the lines of fortification on Barham Downs were the work of armies in more modern times. The earliest account of any military day. The first part of the name " Mercredsburne" was undoubtedly derived from the god Mercred or Mercury. We are told by Cæsar that "the Gauls and Britons worshipped as their divinity 'Mercury' in particular, and have many images of him, and regard him as the inventor of all arts; they consider him the guide of their journeys and marches, and believe him to have very great influence in the acquisition of gain and mercantile transactions." Mercredsburn seems to have been the name of the brook, and Merceredes-burnansted the name of the place near it where the battle was fought. From the latter, the exact locality of this battle may be assigned; for there is a place about a mile and a half distant from the river on its western side, named "Bursted," which may well be an abbreviated form of "Burnansted," and to which tradition has always pointed as the scene of some great battle. The "Mercred" in "Mercredes-burnan-sted has now, it is true, been lost sight of, but it is still, I think, preserved in another form in a locality near at hand called "Hermansole,"—evidently a corruption of "Ermenseul," the name given by the Saxons to the pillars or statues erected to the god "Hermes," the Greek form, as is generally supposed, of "Mercury." This place, Bursted, entirely accords with the description given in the Saxon chronicle, and by Florence of Worcester, both of which accounts state that the battle was fought not *at* but *near* the bank of Mearcredesburn.

tary encampment on these downs since the Norman conquest is thus recorded by Hasted: "On these downs, anno 1213, King John encamped with a mighty army of 60,000 men, to oppose Philip, King of France, who was marching to invade this kingdom; but Pandulph, the Pope's legate, who was then at the house of the Knight's Templars in this neighbourhood, sent two of them to persuade the king to come to him there, where the King, in the presence of his principal nobles and the bishops, resigned his crown to the legate, as the Pope's representative." "Here also, in King Henry III.'s reign, Simon Montford, Earl of Leicester, being declared general of their army by the discontented barons, engaged a numerous army to oppose the landing of Queen Eleanor, whom the king had left behind in France." The downs were also used as a camping-ground in 1642 by the army of the Cavaliers; also in 1760, as appears from the following entry in the Register Book of Burials, in the parish of Bridge: "John Livingstone, a private soldier in Major-General Jeffery's Regiment of Foot (No. 14), who was accidentally killed by a bread or forage waggon belonging to the camp at Barham Downs, going over his body, whereby he was crushed to death. Aug. 17, 1760." In still later times the British troops were also here encamped in preparation for their embarkation for the continent, previous to the battle of Waterloo.

With regard to these various occasions when Barham Downs were occupied by troops, it must be observed that the encampments were only temporary: we have no record of any engagements taking place, or of any escarpments being thrown up for defensive purposes. Barham Downs being within easy reach of the coast, were suitable as a temporary halting-place for troops about to embark for foreign service, or for providing a reserve force in case of the attempted landing of a hostile army; but we have no reason to suppose that any earthworks were thrown up by the troops thus for short periods quartered there. Indeed the defensive strength of the old English barons lay rather in stone walls and castles than in battlements of earth and turf. The fact that these Downs have been used in later years for military purposes, so far from affording any argument against Julius Cæsar having encamped there, points them out rather as the *traditional camping-ground* which, following the example of the Roman conqueror, successive generations employed in times of war.

But we have yet another portion of Cæsar's encampment to describe. The left wing of the Roman army, including the cavalry, advanced, as before-mentioned, in all probability towards the river at Charlton, that being the nearest part of the stream where, after their twelve miles' night-march, they could obtain water for the horses. After the victory of the Roman army on Barham Downs, the greater portion of the left wing was no doubt quartered within the lines of one of the great camps on the downs; but an examination of the declivity between Barham Downs and the river opposite Charlton reveals the traces of three lines of earthworks, each of the length of about three furlongs. Probably Cæsar here quartered his cavalry, in consequence of the proximity to the river. These lines of fortification were perhaps originally thrown up in earlier British wars, but even if they were so, they would doubtless be used by the Romans as an outer line of defence for the camp. It may be noticed also that on the opposite hill, beyond the river, there is a double line of entrenchments, as if of an opposing army. These corresponding entrenchments on each side of the river extend, with greater or less prominence, as far as Kingston Church. There are also two parallel lines of escarpments about 200 yards in length on the brow of the hill in Bourne Park, with others at their extremities, at right angles to them, forming, as it were, a double parapet, one line within the other. They are not at first easily discerned (which argues their great antiquity), but when once noticed, can be plainly made out.

Before quitting Barham Downs and their neighbourhood, it will be well to notice one or two other features, which are corroborative as to their having been the site of Cæsar's camp.

On the brow of the hill, in Bourne Park, there are what appear to be the remains of two outposts, 400 yards apart, surrounded each by a ditch. They are of the same dimensions, and form almost perfect hexagons, each side being about 50 feet in length. They are situated in commanding positions on a hill, called locally "Star Hill," and would afford excellent stations for the guards placed before the gates of the camp, whence they could view the position and movements of the enemy. They are known traditionally as "the Forts." They are now bare of trees, but have the appearance of having been planted at some comparatively recent period.

A deep depression a few yards distant from one of these may possibly have been one of those extemporized amphitheatres with which we know Cæsar sought amusement for his soldiers, when not in actual combat. While Cæsar was ten days absent repairing his vessels, such entertainments would doubtless be resorted to by his soldiery who remained, as we shall hereafter notice, at the camps.

A very formidable stronghold, pointed out by the Ordnance Surveyors on their map as "Roman entrenchments," may be seen at the eastern extremity of the Downs. It is not of Roman but British construction, but may very likely have been used by Cæsar's army as an outpost for the defence of his camp on the extreme left. There appears also to have been a very great mound or tumulus near the south-east corner of the Downs.

On the south-west of Bourne Park there is a noted spring, which is still called " The Roman's Cold Bath." This may have had its origin in Cæsar's time, or subsequently; but we may remark that such a spring, if available, would be much sought for by the soldiers of a stationary camp (castrum stativum) such as Cæsar's was.

With these remarks upon the vestiges still remaining of Cæsar's camp, which, though necessarily imperfect, corroborate, so far as they go, the traditional site on Barham Downs, we pass on to his narrative of the events of the day following his first night of encampment. "Early the day after that day he sent foot soldiers and cavalry in three divisions on an expedition for the purpose of following up those who had fled." This pursuing force corresponded with the three divisions of Cæsar's army, each probably furnishing a contingent, so as not materially to weaken any one division. Three very ancient roads by which they doubtless pursued the retreating

Britons may all be seen from Patrixbourne Hill, the left and central ones in particular being visible at the present day for more than a mile and a half. It is true that in Cæsar's time the country was more thickly wooded than it is now, but these roads passing over chalky soil, and being on rising ground, and converging towards Patrixbourne Hill, would even at that period be readily discerned. We will describe them as they now present themselves to a spectator on the hill. The road on the left hand ascends the steep hill in the direction of Hardres, passing through Whitehill Wood. It leads to an ancient British oppidum in Iffin Wood,[1] a strongly fortified position still known as "the Castle." The central road is now the main road between Canterbury and Dover, and passes through the village of Bridge. It is for a considerable distance identical with the old Roman Watling Street, formerly a British road. The third or right hand road, seen more clearly from Cæsar's

[1] The owner of the property, Mr Bell of Bourne Park, some years ago opened a large tumulus within the enclosure, and dug up British sunburnt pottery and other remains, which showed clearly its British origin.

extreme right wing (consisting of the Coranidæ on the heights of Garrington) than from Patrixbourne Hill, ascends Bekesbourne Hill and enters Canterbury at Longport, while there is yet another road passing through Patrixbourne and Hode (known as the Pilgrims' way), which meets the last mentioned at St Martin's Hill.

There is no doubt of the great antiquity of these roads, and they would naturally be chosen by the Britons for their escape, since they all led to British strongholds, and afforded access to what would be probably their next rallying place, the well-fortified positions at Durovernum and Caer Caint (Canterbury).

CHAPTER VII.

CÆSAR'S RETURN TO THE COAST, AND SUBSEQUENT EVENTS.

CÆSAR'S pursuit of the Britons, which we have described in the previous chapter, was arrested by an unforeseen and serious misfortune. He tells us that when the soldiers ordered for the pursuit "had advanced some portion of their journey, and when already the last were in sight, horsemen came from Quintus Atrius to Cæsar to announce that a great tempest had arisen on the previous night, and that nearly all the vessels had been shattered and cast on shore; that their anchors and cables could no longer hold them, nor could the sailors and masters of the vessels endure the violence of the storm, and that the vessels being driven into collision, great damage had been received."

The news of this disaster reached Cæsar when, as he says, his three pursuing columns "had advanced some portion of their journey, and when now the last were in sight." It has been supposed by some that he intended by this that the last of the fugitive Britons had just come within sight of their pursuers, but the more natural meaning of the passage would be that only the extremities of his own pursuing columns could now be seen from his camp. As we look from Patrixbourne Hill, along the three roads described in the last chapter, we see how the conditions of Cæsar's description of this pursuit are satisfied; for he could see from the hill at Patrixbourne the extreme end of the columns sent in pursuit, as they defiled over the opposite hill, for a mile or a mile and a half. Beyond this distance he would be unable to see them, for, having gained the height of the hill, they would begin to descend into the lower ground beyond it.

The terrible disaster which had happened to

his ships would have daunted a general less brave and experienced than Cæsar. But his resolution was at once taken. "These things being known," he says, "Cæsar orders the legions and the cavalry to be recalled, and to desist from the journey. He himself returns to his vessels; he perceives in person almost the same things that he had learned from messengers and by letters,— namely, that with the loss of about forty vessels the rest could probably be repaired by great efforts. He chooses therefore artificers from the legions, and orders others to be brought over from the continent." Now it is not to be supposed, although many have assumed that he did so, that Cæsar returned to the coast with his whole army. He nowhere says that he did, and there were many reasons against such a course. He would have lost all the ground he had gained, and would besides have tempted the Britons to have attacked his rear. When it is said that he ordered the legions and cavalry to be recalled, and to desist from their journey, the reference is plainly to those foot soldiers and cavalry who were on their journey in pursuit of the routed enemy. He says that he himself, no doubt with a sufficient force for his own protection, returned to the coast, and chose artificers from the legions for the repair of his ships. It must be remembered that the extremity of Cæsar's encampments on Barham Downs was only twelve Roman miles (about eleven and one-third English miles) from the strand at Deal, and that he could easily send that distance for the artificers he required. Nor would it be likely that Cæsar, having after a hard struggle gained the vantage ground of these hills for his camp, would readily relinquish it, and thus allow the Britons to reoccupy their former positions. No necessity for such a course had arisen. Cæsar had left 5000 men, besides his naval brigade (probably 5000), in charge of his vessels, and no doubt took with him on his return to the coast a considerable force including the artificers. These, with others which he says were brought over from the continent, would suffice to throw up his naval camp and haul up his vessels, especially as they were employed for ten days and nights in the work. He certainly would not have required his whole army for the purpose, and it is much more reasonable to suppose that the main portion of Cæsar's army on Barham Downs and his allies at Garrington, thoroughly fortified the camp (and the traces of entrenchments already described bear out the supposition), so as to protect themselves from all hostile attacks during Cæsar's ten days' absence.[1]

In place of the forty vessels which were destroyed by the storm, Cæsar orders others to be built on the continent. "He writes to Labienus that he should build as many vessels as he could with the help of those legions which were with him. He himself, although it was a work of much toil and trouble, determines that it would be most advantageous that all the vessels should be drawn on shore and be united with the camp by one fortification. In these measures he spends about ten days, the labours of the soldiers being not even relaxed during the night."

The labour of thus hauling his vessels on shore

---

[1] In this we are confirmed by the opinion of Camden, who says that Cæsar "kept his men encamped for ten days, till he had refitted his fleet, shattered very much by a tempest, and got it to shore."

must have been immense, but Cæsar had the example of others to guide him, for the feat was not now accomplished for the first time. Homer relates that, when the Greeks had landed on the coast of Troy, the ships were drawn on land, and fastened at the poop to large stones, attached to ropes, which served as anchors. The Greeks then surrounded the fleet with a fortification to secure it against the attacks of the enemy. It is recorded also by Herodotus, Thucydides, and others, that in cases where it would have been necessary to coast round a considerable extent of country connected with the mainland by a narrow neck, the ships were sometimes drawn across the neck of land from the one sea to the other by machines called ολκοι (olkoi). This was done not unfrequently across the Isthmus of Corinth.

But to continue Cæsar's history. "The vessels," he relates, "having been drawn up, and the camp excellently fortified,[1] he leaves the same forces which he left before as a guard to

[1] The vestiges of his naval camp mentioned by Camden, Leland, and others, and still to some extent visible, have been described in a former chapter.

the ships, and proceeded to the same place whence he had returned. When he had come thither greater forces of the Britons had assembled at that place from all parts." It is evident from this account that his camp at Barham Downs was seriously threatened during his absence, news probably having reached the British chiefs of the loss he had sustained at the coast. The strength of his camp on the downs had prevented any attack being as yet made upon it, but a long line, sometimes a double line of entrenchments, still traceable about half a mile from the foot of the hills from Garrington to Charlton, remains in proof that the Britons had not been idle. Here doubtless they took up their defensive position on the western side of the stream during Cæsar's absence, not venturing, after their former experience, to attack the camp, but awaiting the course of events, while Cæsar had ordered his own men to remain in their entrenched position till his return.

The Britons had an able general, by whose advice they seem to have proceeded cautiously in their future engagements with the Roman army.

Cæsar mentions him now for the first time, though it is certain that he had from the commencement of the war been their leader. "The chief command and management of the war," he says, "was entrusted by common consent to Cassivellaunus, whose territories the river called Thames divides from the maritime states at about eighty miles from the sea. In former time continual warfare had waged between him and the other states, but on our arrival the Britons, moved with fear, had given this man chief command of military affairs."

Several succeeding chapters of Cæsar's "Commentaries" are occupied with a digression on the geography, manners, and customs of the Britons. Many of his remarks on these subjects have been introduced from time to time according as they seemed to illustrate our narrative. We pass on, therefore, to chapter xv., where the history of his progress in Britain is resumed.

"The horse and chariotmen of the enemy engaged," he says, "in sharp combat with our cavalry on their journey; not but that our men, however, were superior everywhere, and drove them into the woods and hills."

It seems uncertain whether Cæsar is here referring to attacks made upon the force he had with him on his return from the coast, or to the battles fought afterwards in his further progress. It is very likely that he was molested to some extent on his return journey from his naval camp, for the Britons had doubtless many oppida [1] near his line of march, and several kings, some of whose names are afterwards mentioned in the history, and who carried on a guerilla warfare with him. But, as Cæsar has told us that on his return to his camp (on Barham Downs), he found the enemy gathered *there* in large numbers, we may infer that he did not meet with any very serious opposition till he arrived there. On his arrival, however, at his camp, and after resting the troops he had brought back with him, he would appear to have lost no time in displacing the Britons from the positions they had taken up. The "Cambrian history" relates that "to guard the camp, Cæsar stationed 10,000 men with the two first cohorts of the seventh and ninth legions. The rest of his army, consisting of 35,000 legionaries, 3000 cavalry, and 20,000 Coranidæ under Avarwy, he drew up

[1] Traces of oppida remain at Coldred, Kingston, and Atchester.

in three divisions on a declivity, called in 'the Triads' 'the green spot.' The British army occupied the open ground opposite, its left wing under Nennius, resting on a marsh." We are led to suppose from this account that Cæsar, leaving 10,000 men in his camp, now advanced and took up his position in three divisions on the brow of the hill. A line of embankment is still traceable along the brow of the hill in several places, especially between Patrixbourne and Bekesbourne, and at Bishopsbourne—indicating the positions which the advanced guards of his three divisions probably took up, and, as we have already noticed, there are corresponding lines of entrenchment of the Britons, about half a mile from the foot of the hill on the other side of the stream. A desperate encounter here took place, as Cæsar himself admits. His cavalry, as was natural, were the first to attack They were strenuously resisted by the cavalry and chariotmen of the enemy, and although Cæsar's forces still advanced and drove the Britons into the woods and hills, yet he records some casualties among his own men. Very many (of the enemy) having been killed, our men lost some of their own, from having pursued too eagerly. Yet they, after an interval, rushed suddenly from the woods, our men being taken unawares and being occupied in the fortification of the camp; and an attack having been made on those who were placed in station before the camp, there was a sharp encounter, and two cohorts (and those the first of two legions) having been sent in aid by Cæsar, when they had stopped, with a very small interval between them (our men being terrified by the unaccustomed mode of warfare), the enemy burst forth with great boldness through their midst, and retired thence unharmed. On that day Quintus Laberius Durus was slain, but the enemy was driven back, more cohorts having been sent in aid."

It would appear from the foregoing narrative that notwithstanding the desperate opposition they met with, the Roman army had made sufficient progress to have chosen an advanced camp, which they were fortifying when the Britons rushed out upon them from the woods. May not this new camp have been the strong British oppidum in Iffin Wood, about three miles distant from their former camp on Barham Downs? In the kind of guerilla warfare which the British adopted, it was necessary for the Romans to dispossess them from their strongholds, " to drive them," as Cæsar puts it "from the woods," where their oppida were situated. This particular oppidum was very strongly entrenched, and the Romans by possessing themselves of it would obtain a very strong position for their advanced camp, and one which we can easily understand the Britons would make every effort to retake. There are indeed indications of its having been held by Roman soldiers at some time or another; for a long straight line of outer entrenchment, in the shape of a Roman agger and ditch, still remains at a short distance from the British oppidum, at the side of the Roman road called "Stone Street."

The extent of the advance made by the Roman army during this day's continuous fighting is indicated by the tradition which assigns to Chilham the tomb of Laberius. Although doubt is thrown upon this traditional account by Archdeacon Batteley, the locality so entirely agrees with the limit which our history would have claimed for Cæsar's advance that we are inclined to accept it.

It may be observed in conclusion that a victorious result of the day's conflict is claimed by both sides. The Cambrian history says that "the Romans were towards evening driven from their camp, but the success of the day was dearly purchased by the death of Nennius, who fell in the last onset of the retreating enemy."

The British account refers to the combat of the right wing of the Roman army, consisting principally of the Coranidæ under Avarwy, with the Britons led by Nennius. The Roman historian, on the other hand, having regard principally to the victory of the left wing and centre of Cæsar's army, claims the day for the Romans. Possibly both accounts are substantially correct. It is clear, however, from Cæsar's own narrative that his army had not gained a decisive victory. The enemy, after greatly disordering the Roman cohorts and inflicting upon them the loss of a tribune (Laberius Durus), were only at last repulsed by a strong reinforcement. Cæsar makes mention of their skilful management of their chariots in this battle, for observing which the elevated position which he occupied on the hill at **Patrixbourne** afforded him a good opportunity. "In the whole of this kind of battle," he says, "since it was contested under the eyes of all and before the camp, it was perceived that our men, on account of the weight of their arms (inasmuch as they could neither follow those who were giving way, nor dared to depart from their standards), were little suited for an enemy of this kind; that the cavalry moreover fought with great danger, because that they (the enemy) would ofttimes retreat even designedly, and when they had drawn off our horse a little way from the legions, would leap down from their chariots and fight on foot in unequal combat. But the system of cavalry engagement is wont to bring equal danger, and of the same kind both to those retreating and those pursuing." To this was added, "that the enemy never fought in close order, but in small parties, and at considerable distances, and had detachments placed about (in different parts), and some in turn took the place of others, and the vigorous and fresh succeeded those who were wearied."

The day following the Britons endeavoured to renew the tactics which they had found successful on the previous day. "They took up their position at a distance from the camp, on the hills, and began to show themselves in small parties, and with less spirit than on the day before, to provoke our horsemen to combat." It does not, however, appear from this statement of "the Commentaries" that Cæsar accepted the challenge to renew the contest. He recognised the necessity of occupying his troops in what must have become a work of no little difficulty in a country where he could carry on no barter with the inhabitants, namely, the provisioning of his large army. At noon, therefore, he sent out three legions and all the cavalry with C. Trebonius, the lieutenant, for the purpose of foraging. He was probably led to suppose by the want of vigour with which the small parties of the enemy manœuvred, that their main forces had withdrawn themselves to a distance. Soon, however, he was undeceived. They were concealed, doubtless, in the strongly fortified oppidum at Durovernum, and in the neighbouring woods; and now that the Roman legions, thrown off their guard, were scattered throughout the fields, "they flew," writes Cæsar, "upon the foragers suddenly from all quarters, so that they did not hold off even from the standards and legions. Our men, making a fierce attack upon them, repulsed them; nor did they cease from pursuing them until the horse, confident of support, since they saw the legions behind them, drove the enemy headlong, and slaying a great number of them, gave them no opportunity either of rallying or halting, or of leaping down from their chariots."

Whither did the fugitive Britons escape? The description of their rout would lead to the supposition that they fled, not at once into their woods and oppida, but along their principal chariot roads, making all haste to escape from their fierce pursuers; and since it is stated that the Roman cavalry, knowing that the legions were behind them, pursued them with confidence, it seems probable that the Britons fled for the most part in *one direction*. It may also be concluded that they escaped by a *road* in an exactly opposite direction to that which led to the Roman encampments on Barham Downs, namely, by their principal military road,[1] the Sarn Gwyddelin, or Irish Road, afterwards the Roman Watling Street. It is related by Geoffrey of Monmouth that Cassivellaunus, being defeated in the battle, fled with his disordered forces to a rocky hill, on the top of which was a thick hazel wood, and that he defended the hill with such bravery and obstinacy that Cæsar could only dislodge him by besieging the place for two days, after which, compelled by famine, Cassivellaunus submitted himself to his great conqueror. The details of this story must be rejected as altogether inconsistent with Cæsar's narrative; but that the Britons, followed in hot pursuit by the victorious Roman cavalry and legions, found at length a temporary refuge in

[1] The Romans laid down their military vias, wherever they could, upon the foundations of the previously existing British roads. The British chroniclers claim that the principal military roads (many of them known afterwards as Roman roads) of the country were the work of Dunwallo Molmutius (Dyvnwal Moelmud), their great lawgiver, and that, being completed by his son, Belinus, they were called the Belinian Roads. The rapidity with which the British chariots moved from one point to another (see page 129) proves that these roads were well made and maintained.

some stronghold, whence they were with difficulty dislodged by Cæsar, is not improbable. That there was some such foundation for the story seems to be justified by a tradition which assigns to a hill near Newington, about eighteen miles from Canterbury, the name of Key Coll or Caius' (Julius Cæsar's) hill.

The disastrous results of this day's combat thoroughly disheartened the brave British allies. Cassivellaunus experienced the humiliating fortune of all unsuccessful generals, namely, the falling away of his auxiliary forces. "Immediately after this retreat," says Cæsar, "the auxiliaries who had assembled from all sides departed; nor after that time did the enemy ever engage with us in very large numbers."

The British resistance from this time consisted for the most part of a guerilla warfare, harassing, no doubt, to Cæsar's disciplined forces, but not affording any prospect of a successful result. Cæsar relates that, "*discovering their design*, he led his army into the territories of Cassivellaunus to the river Thames." It must be remembered that Cæsar wrote after the event; the design, therefore, which he professes to have discovered must be interpreted by the after history. It was, in the first place, to hasten forward with his main forces in order to prevent his passage of the Thames, and meanwhile to weaken his legions by attacking them when foraging in isolated parties in the fields.

From this point the identification of Cæsar's progress to the Thames with actual localities becomes practically impossible. His history of events is somewhat confused. No distances are recorded, nor the number of days occupied in his journeys from place to place. He was frequently harassed by small parties of Britons, from whom his cavalry especially suffered, but never really confronted by any serious opposition.

There can be little doubt, however, as to the route which he took in his journey to the Thames. He had with him Avarwy, from whom he would learn that the Gwyddelin road was the usual and direct route to the river Thames, and moreover passed through a comparatively open country, in which his army would be less likely to be disturbed by sudden irruptions of the enemy from the woods.

We have no data whereby we can assign with certainty the various halting-places of Cæsar's army; but the fortified positions of the Britons, which he doubtless occupied along the Gwyddelin road, and which it is probable afterwards became Roman military stations, have a strong claim to be regarded as the sites of his temporary encampments. Some of these, named in "the Itinerary" of Antoninus, may, I think, be identified with actual localities, although their distances from one another are not in all cases exactly the same [1] as those given by Antoninus.

[1] Many writers have attempted to reconcile the differences between the distances of "the Itinerary," and the actual distances between places mentioned by Antoninus. An explanation worthy of notice is given by Horsley, who supposes that the Romans measured the horizontal distances from place to place without regard to the inequalities of the surface; so that on undulating ground the distances given by Antoninus would be less than the actual measurements along the roads. For instance, on the hilly road between Dover and Canterbury, which Antoninus makes to be fourteen Roman miles (equal to about thirteen and one-third English miles) apart, there is a difference of nearly three miles between this measurement and the real distance along the road, which is sixteen miles. Even this explanation, however, will not reconcile the differences in all cases, and the most reasonable conclusion seems to be, that some of the distances

After the battle, which we have supposed to have terminated with the final struggle at Key Coll, it is probable that Cæsar (though still holding the hill) encamped his troops a little further back along the Gwyddelin Road, namely, at Bapchild, which I think was the ancient Durolevum.[1] He must have traversed with

given by Antoninus have been altered by transcribers, since we find that some of the numerals vary in different editions of "the Itinerary." One other explanation, however, may be suggested, namely, that although we may be able to identify most of the Roman stations mentioned in "the Itinerary" with modern towns, we do not know from what particular place in each town Antoninus measured his journeys. He probably commenced from the extremity of the Roman settlement, which may have been in some cases a mile or two outside the modern town.

[1] Gibson, Camden's annotator, after objecting that Lenham, where Camden has placed Durolevum, did not suit well with the distance given by Antoninus of that place from Durovernum (Canterbury), observes, "What then if we should pitch upon Bapchild, a place lying between Sittingbourne and Ospringe, the ancient name whereof is Baccanceld, afterwards corrupted into Beck-child, and now corruptly called Bapchild. For as *Dur* (in British) denotes *water*, so *Bec* in the Saxon answers to that; or at least the termination *celd*, implying a *pool*, will in some measure suit the old name. But what is of more consequence in this matter, is its being in the Saxon times a place of very great note; insomuch that

his army, during that hard day's fighting and pursuit of the Britons, a distance of more than twenty miles. From Bapchild to Rochester (Durobrovis), which was the next Roman station, is a distance of about twelve miles, and it may well be imagined that, after the great exertions of his army the previous day, Cæsar would be

Bishop Brightwald, A.D. 700, held a Synod at it. Now, 'tis a general remark made by antiquaries, that the Saxons particularly fixed upon those places where the Romans had left their *stations;* from whence at present so many of our towns end in Chester. And even at this day here are the ruins of two old churches or chapels, besides the parish church. Moreover, if the Roman Road, betwixt the Kentish towns, was the same with the present, then Durolevum (which, by the way, is only read Durolenum, to reconcile it to Lenham) must be somewhere about this parish; because no other place in the present road is so agreeable a distance between the said cities. Now there cannot be a shorter cut between Rochester and Canterbury, than that at present is, unless one should level hills or travel through bogs; and yet by this the distance between is about 25 miles, the same with the Itinerary (Iter. 2 and 4), as also where Durolevum comes between, 13 to it from Rochester, and 12 from it to Canterbury, makes exactly the same number."

It may be added that the valuable collection of Roman pottery and glass, dug up by Mr George Payne, jun., of Sittingbourne, in this immediate neighbourhood, affords further presumptive evidence that the ancient Durolevum was at Bapchild.

content with this short progress, and make at Rochester his next encampment. Mr C. Roach Smith, whose residence at Strood (near Rochester) has afforded him opportunities of observing the ancient bed of the river, and of the Swale into which it flows, is of opinion that the river Medway passing through Rochester would, at the time of Julius Cæsar, present no difficulty to his progress, being fordable at low water, or easily bridged over.

In his valuable "Retrospections,"[1] of which the first two volumes have been published, he writes, speaking of the low-lying land to the south of the Medway, called "the Upchurch Marshes,"— "These marshes are an interesting study for the geologist as well as the antiquary. When the Romans inhabited and worked the land, it lay high and dry, and the Medway must have been confined within comparatively narrow limits. It was probably some time after the Romans had left before the sea began to make inroads and submerge hundreds of acres." Mr R. Smith has discovered large quantities of Roman pottery by digging in

[1] "Retrospections, Social and Archæological," by C. Roach Smith, Esq., F.S.A.

the creeks of the marshes, and in the river at low water; and he says that there was time enough for the earth to accumulate two or three feet over the débris of the kilns, ere the creeks formed, and washed the remains into their beds, where they are now found.

After crossing the Medway, Cæsar would no doubt have pursued his journey by the Gwyddelin road until he reached the Thames[1]

[1] I am confirmed in this statement by the opinion, kindly communicated to me, of Mr Roach Smith, that the modern road from Dover to London runs upon the Roman military via, and that this was constructed upon the remains of the ancient British road. The idea which formerly prevailed, that the Roman road was diverted from its direct course in consequence of the marshes about Deptford forming a large lake or lagoon, has been disproved by recent researches. An interesting paper in the "Archæological Journal" for 1885, by Mr F. C. J. Spurrell, enters fully into this subject. Mr Spurrell shows that a yew forest, of which the stubs may still be seen at 12 feet below the present high-water mark, stretched over the whole of the marshes at Deptford, Dagenham, Rainham, Erith, and Plumstead. He also states that Roman bricks and pottery have been discovered in these marshes, and the remains of Roman dwellings, both at Westminster (in digging the foundations of the Canon's residences) and at Southwark; —in every case several feet below the present high-water mark. In fact, the whole of Roman London was built on a much lower level than the modern city. Sir Christopher Wren (see Noorthouck's "History of London"), in digging the foundations

had there been any means of transit for his army at the point where the road met that river. Mr Morgan indeed asserts, on the authority of some British account, that the Romans followed this road, but found upon arriving at the river that the bridge between Belins' Tower and the southern bank of the Thames was broken down, and that consequently they were compelled to cross the river at its nearest fordable place. This statement, although I think it cannot be sustained, it will be well to examine.

There are certainly some grounds for the supposition that there may have been a bridge over the Thames at the period of our history.

The fact that the Britons endeavoured to prevent the passage of Cæsar's army, where it afterwards crossed the Thames by wooden piles driven into the bed of the river, shows that they could easily have formed one; and

for the Church of St Mary-le-Bow, Cheapside, found a Roman causeway, four feet thick, made of rough stone and Roman brick, 18 feet below the level of the present city.

These facts show that the Thames could not have been at the time of the Roman occupation so considerable a river as it is at the present day.

they must have understood the construction of bridges, since Cæsar, in his Belgic war, crossed the river Aisne by a bridge; and he himself tells us that the southern portion of Britain was largely peopled from Belgium. The rapidity with which bridges were made at the period of our history would surprise even the engineers of our own day. Cæsar relates that he formed a bridge of wooden piles over the Rhine (probably at Bonn), for the passage of his army in the short space of ten days, including the time occupied in the conveyance of the timber. A century later, when Aulus Plautius crossed the Thames, the Germans in his army swam the river at its mouth, "where," as Dion states, "by the flowing of the tide it stagnates," but the rest of his troops crossed at a higher part of the river by bridges (possibly a bridge of boats). Mr Beale Poste thinks that the river thus crossed was the Lea, a tributary of the Thames, rather than the Thames itself, but Dion Cassius' history of the event affords no ground for such a supposition. On the contrary, he relates that having crossed the Thames, Plautius sent for the Emperor Claudius, and having awaited his arrival,—probably at the strongly fortified position of Keston in Kent,—he gave over the command of the army to the Emperor, who crossed the river, and having conquered the enemy, took Camulodunum (Colchester, in Essex), the royal seat of Cunobellin. Whether this bridge, over which Plautius, and afterwards his royal master, crossed, existed previously, or whether it was temporarily thrown over the river by the Roman soldiers, we have no means of deciding, but the mention of it suggests the possibility that only a century after Julius Cæsar's invasion of the country, the Britons had constructed, or reconstructed, a bridge across the river.[1]

[1] We have no record that the Romans, during their occupation of the country, used any other means of transit over the Thames than a trajectus of wood. Mr Roach Smith, however (see "Illustrations of Roman London"), has discovered indications of the existence of a Roman bridge on the site of old London Bridge. Great quantities of Roman coins and antiquities were brought up from the bed of the river when foundations of the old bridge were taken down, while the houses there were generally built on piles, showing that the ground had been gained from the river. The Saxon

While, however, these arguments may be urged in favour of the British account that Cæsar proceeded to the Thames, expecting to find a bridge by which his army could cross the river, they are outweighed by the fact that Cæsar makes no allusion to this in his "Commentaries." He would naturally be reluctant to mention any failure of his designs, but he could scarcely omit all reference to such a manifest discomfiture of his plans, since it would have been witnessed by his whole army. We are led, therefore, to the conclusion that he diverged from the Gwyddelin road at some point after passing Rochester in order to reach that part of the river where he had learnt from Avarwy it was fordable. The road he followed probably led to what was afterwards the Roman station Noviomagus. This is generally believed to have been at Holwood Hill.

chroniclers do not make mention of the existence of a bridge across the Thames at London until A.D. 1017, when Cnut (or Canute), the Dane, invading London with a fleet, to dispossess Edmund Ironside, found himself unable to pass the bridge over the river at London, which the citizens had strongly fortified. He consequently cut a canal on the south side of the river, deep and broad enough to convey ships above the bridge.

near Keston,[1] which is in a direct line between London and Maidstone (probably the Roman station called Vagniacæ), and agrees fairly well with the distances of Noviomagus from those towns in "the Itinerary." The name "Keston," Hasted thinks, is derived from "Chesterton," *i.e.*, "the place of the Camp, or Fortification," though some fancy that it is a corruption of "Kæsar's town." Many Roman remains and foundations with coins of the middle and lower Empires have been discovered there, and the extensive fortifications, nearly two miles in circumference, and existing in parts of ramparts and double ditches, prove it to have been a large Roman encampment.

From this place Cæsar would reach, in less than a day's march, the fordable part of the

[1] Crayford, on the Watling Street, or Gwyddelin Road, has by many learned authors been identified with Noviomagus. It is about the right distance both from London and Maidstone, although not in a direct line between them. Its manor, says Hasted, is called "Newbury," which signifies the same as "Noviomagus," namely, "the new fortress, or station." Its claims to have been a Roman station are not, however, supported by any considerable discoveries of Roman antiquities. Mr Spurrell says that a quarter of a mile south of Howbury there is the barest outline of an oval camp.

Thames. His passage of the river was not unchallenged. Cassivellaunus, with his chariots and Essedarii, of whom he still retained 4000, had anticipated his arrival. When Cæsar arrived there "he perceived," so his "Commentaries" relate, "that numerous forces of the enemy were marshalled on the other bank of the river; the bank also was defended by sharp stakes fixed in front, and stakes of the same kind fixed under the water were covered by the river." The Roman general, however, knew the resolution and bravery of his own soldiers; "discovering these things from prisoners and deserters, sending forward the cavalry, he ordered the legions to follow them immediately. With such speed and eagerness did the soldiers advance, though they stood up to their heads in the water, that the enemy could not sustain the attacks of the legions and of the horse, but quitted the banks and betook themselves to flight."[1]

[1] The story of Polyænus that Cæsar employed an elephant on this occasion, which struck such terror by its novel appearance, that the Britons fled in all directions, is unsupported by any other testimony.

The particular place where the Roman army crossed the Thames has been the subject of much dispute. Tradition, however, again helps us to a conclusion. The part of the river known as "Coway Stakes" by its very name is pointed out as the place where Cæsar's forces forded the stream. Even in Bede's time (A.D. 730) the stakes fixed by the Britons were still visible, and, remaining there for so many centuries, undoubtedly gave the name to the place. Bede thus describes them and their origin, according to the tradition extant in his day. Cæsar "proceeded to the river Thames, where an immense multitude of the enemy had posted themselves on the farther side of the river, under the command of Cassivellaunus, and fenced the bank of the river and almost all the ford under water, with sharp stakes, the remains of which are to be seen to this day, each apparently about the thickness of a man's thigh, and being cased with lead, were fixed immoveably in the bottom of the river." Camden has no hesitation in assigning to this locality the passage of the great conqueror. "'Tis impossible," he says, "I should be mistaken in the place, because here the river is scarce six foot deep, and the place, at this day, from those *stakes* is called Coway *Stakes*; to which add that Cæsar makes the bounds of Cassivellaun, where he settles this passage of his, to be about 80 miles distant from that sea which washes the east part of Kent, where he landed. Now this ford, we mention, is at the same distance from the sea; and I am the first that I know of that has mentioned and settled it in its proper place."

The subsequent progress of Cæsar may be briefly narrated. After passing the Thames, he advanced against the stronghold of Cassivellaunus, generally supposed to have been at Verulam (St Albans), harassed continually on the way by the chariotmen of the enemy, who, from their knowledge of the roads and paths, were able to make unexpected attacks upon his soldiers while occupied in devastating the country. Meanwhile the influence of Avarwy (Mandubratius) with the Trinobantes (the inhabitants of Middlesex), over whom his father, and probably he himself, had formerly ruled, obtained for Cæsar the submission of that people; and other neighbouring tribes, seeing the protection afforded by Cæsar to the Trinobantes, soon after sent in their allegiance to him.

The oppidum of Cassivellaunus was now attacked. It was surrounded by woods and marshes, and well fortified both by nature and art. Cæsar assaulted it on two sides, and although its defenders made a brief but gallant stand, dispirited and outnumbered, they soon fled from the stronghold, and very many of them were cut down in their flight. A large number of cattle was found there; of which Cæsar makes special mention, as the provisioning of his army had no doubt been a matter of considerable difficulty.

One final struggle of the gallant British nation against the invaders of their country was, however, yet to be made in Kent. It will be remembered that, after the defeat of the Britons at Key Coll, the auxiliary forces of Cassivellaunus were dispersed. Those who remained with him were probably the forces he had brought from his own tribe, and others north of the Thames. Finding, however, the desperate straits to which he was reduced, Cassivellaunus made one more attempt to rally the people of Kent. He sent messengers to the four kings of Kent, Cingetorix, Carnilius, Taximagulus, and Segonax, enjoining them to gather all their forces, and make a sudden attack upon Cæsar's naval camp, hoping, no doubt, by this expedient to compel Cæsar to return at once to the coast. His orders were obeyed, but the spirit which still animated the Britons to rise at the call of duty was invoked in vain. The attack upon Cæsar's naval camp was unsuccessful. The well-disciplined Romans who defended it, made a sortie in full force from the camp. Cingetorix was taken prisoner, and the defeated Britons many of them slain.

The news of this disaster decided Cassivellaunus to seek for terms of peace. "So many losses having been received, his territories devastated, and being distressed most of all by the defection of the states, he sends ambassadors to Cæsar to treat, through Comius the Atrebatian, concerning a surrender."

Cæsar wishing to pass the winter on the continent, and the summer being now nearly past, demanded hostages of Cassivellaunus, and an annual tribute to be paid to the Roman people. Having received the hostages, and enjoined Cassivellaunus not to wage war against Mandubratius or the Trinobantes, he led his army back to the sea. There he found his ships repaired, and caused them to be launched. His numerous prisoners, and the fact that some of his ships had been lost in the storm, compelled him to carry back his army to the continent in two convoys. In this he met with some disappointment. Although none of the ships which bore his troops were lost, yet the greater part of those which were returning empty after landing the first convoy, and most of those which Labienus had, to the number of sixty, provided, did not reach their destination, being driven back by contrary winds to the continent. Cæsar, having waited for them for some time in vain, and fearing from the approach of the equinox that the time for safe sailing would soon be past, decided to pack his soldiers more closely than usual into the vessels that remained to him. Taking advantage therefore of calm weather, he set sail at the beginning of the second watch (9 P.M.), and after a favourable passage, landed all his vessels in safety on the continent at day-break.[1] Thus ended an expedition, which, for the boldness of its design, and the undaunted energy with which it was carried through, has not perhaps been surpassed in the history of the world. It has been our aim to trace the footsteps of the conqueror through that part of England on which he landed. His place of disembarkation and the *earlier* part of his progress have, we trust, been established clearly in these pages, and, so far as reasonable conjecture can serve as a guide, his subsequent advance to the Thames has been pointed out. Beyond this we do not attempt to define his route, or to decide whether Verulam, or, as some say,

---

[1] Cæsar, according to his own statement, set sail shortly before the equinox (September 26th). This accords well with a letter of Cicero, in which he says, "On the 11th of the calends of November (October 17th), I received letters from my brother Quintus and from Cæsar; the expedition was finished and the hostages delivered. They had made no booty; they had only imposed contributions. The letters, written from the shores of Britain, are dated on the 6th of the calends of October (September 21st), at the moment of embarking the army which they are bringing back." Cæsar then left Britain on September 21st, having stayed on the island about sixty days.

Wendover was the stronghold of his great opponent. It may be for others to take up the narrative who have greater local knowledge of the country through which he afterwards passed. So far as we have been able to do so, it has been a pleasant recreation both to follow the footsteps of so great a hero as Cæsar, and to place on record in clearer light the exploits of our brave forefathers. Enough, if we have done anything to elucidate a page of our country's history, which has hitherto been much obscured.

APPENDIX.

RESPECTING RICHBOROUGH, AND ITS CLAIM TO BE THE LANDING PLACE OF JULIUS CÆSAR.

ALTHOUGH Deal so entirely answers to the description given by Cæsar of his landing place, that there can be no doubt but that he disembarked his troops at that place, Richborough, the ancient Rutupium, is certainly a formidable rival, and has found very able advocacy from many,[1] and especially from the learned antiquary, Archdeacon Batteley. His arguments deserve consideration in these pages, not only on account of the weight which attaches to his authority, but on account of the challenge, as it were, thrown down to those who advance the claims of Deal. His work, written in Latin, and published in 1711, is in the form of a dialogue between himself and his two friends, Wharton and Maurice. It will be sufficient to summarize the arguments by which he seeks to establish that Richborough was the landing-place of Julius Cæsar.

He argues first from the alleged suitableness of the place

---

[1] The most recent advocate for Rutupium is Mr George Dowker, whose paper, published in the "Journal of the Archæological Institute," vol. xxxiii., is valuable on account of the attention he has given to the geological changes of the coast and of the river Stour.

itself; the facilities it afforded for the landing and provisioning of troops, its proximity to the continent, and the ready means of retreat it afforded to an army harassed by the enemy. Let us consider how these advantages bear upon the question of Cæsar's landing.

That Richborough and its harbour became, after the time of Julius Cæsar, celebrated in history may be readily conceded. No one who has visited the remains of its ancient Roman castle, within whose walls King Ethelbert held his court, and where he received St Augustine and his monks; no one who has stood over the cross on which the ancient chapel was afterwards built, and where Christianity began to send forth afresh its blessings through our country, would wish to deny to Richborough any honour that rightly belongs to it. It was probably the first stone-built stronghold in England, and it is marvellous, especially considering that its walls have no solid foundation, that it has stood through so many ages of wars and invasions. The Saxon, the Dane, the Norman have assailed its battlements or have found refuge within its walls. Still the old castle stands, a ruin of its former self, battered about by time and war, yet not destroyed; the circumference of its walls complete or nearly so, its gates still remaining, amongst them the decuman or ancient skaian gate, with its oblique entrance, the scene doubtless of many a conflict and many a deed of bravery. Batteley is probably right in saying that the foundation of its walls dates from the time of Aulus Plautius, though doubtless they owed much to the labours of successive generations, and especially to the Emperor Severus, who, it is said, built the neighbouring castle at Reculver.

But why did Richborough and the Rutupian harbour become of such importance as to need such a defence as this?

APPENDIX. 235

For the same reason, we reply, that Malta and Gibraltar are of such importance to us now; because they commanded the water-way of nations. The narrow stream, now separating the isle of Thanet from the mainland, was formerly an arm of the sea some miles in breadth.[1] Large vessels traversed its waters, bringing the merchandise of many lands to the great port of London, for, as Batteley says, the river Thames continued to give its name to the waters which flowed through the Wantsum, and claimed for itself the sea coast as far as Dover.[2] Richborough, strongly fortified, held the key of this the nearest and most commodious route to London.

But the question for our consideration is, had Richborough this importance at the time of Julius Cæsar's invasion? What was the condition of Richborough and the Portus Rutupinus at that period? Batteley himself tells us that Richborough was an island. "I think, indeed," he says, "that Rutupium was neither in the Isle of Thanet nor in Britain, but in an island of its own, which the Wantsum made near its eastern mouth; since the marshy and low plain by which the field of

---

[1] It was called the Wantsum, a Saxon word meaning, according to Batteley, "valde decrescens." Hasted says that "it was once in its widest part four miles across, but it had by degrees retired so much, that even in the Venerable Bede's time it was but three furlongs over, and was usually passable at two places only; these were Sarre and Stonar, where two ferry-boats were kept for that purpose. It was navigable throughout so late as the time of King Henry VIII., for Twyne, who lived in the latter part of that reign, tells us that there were people then living who had often seen vessels of good burthen pass to and fro upon it, where the water was then, especially towards the west, totally excluded; all which, he adds, happened because the fresh streams were not sufficient to check the salt water that choked up the channel."

[2] The rights of pilotage still exercised by the Trinity House pilots as far as Dover are a remnant of this ancient claim.

Rutupium is on all sides surrounded, proves to any one contemplating the situation of the place, that it was formerly surrounded by water." A visit to Richborough will confirm the opinion Batteley here expresses. The castle of Richborough was evidently built on an island comparatively small in size, separated from the mainland by a channel of considerable width. The low level of the surrounding country proves that the southern bank of this channel and of the Wantsum must have been a morass, covered by the waves at high water; at low water stagnant, and in many places impassable. Was this, we ask, a favourable situation for the landing of Cæsar's large army? Aulus Plautius no doubt found the island itself suitable as a place of garrison, in the rear of his advancing army, and the Rutupian harbour would afford safe anchorage for his fleet. But Julius Cæsar could not have landed on an island, for he marched, on the occasion of his second invasion, twelve miles inland on the very day of disembarking his troops; nor could so small an island as Richborough have afforded accommodation for the encampment of his legions.

Are we then to suppose that so experienced a general as Julius Cæsar brought his vessels to the marshy shore of the Rutupian straits, when he himself tells us, with evident satisfaction, that he chose an open and level shore for landing, and when he is entirely silent as to the almost insuperable difficulties which he would have encountered had he attempted to land on a morass? Batteley, however, brings forward his authorities to prove that Cæsar did so land, although he confesses that he cannot reconcile their statements with Cæsar's own narrative. His witnesses are Plutarch and Dion Cassius. Let us see what weight attaches to their authority, as against that of Cæsar himself. The statement of Plutarch, on which Batteley relies, is that relating to the exploit (recorded in chapter iv.) of one of Cæsar's soldiers in Britain, when his captains were "driven into a marsh or bog full of mire and dirt." Now, apart from the fact that the incident he relates is somewhat similar to one recorded by Valerius Maximus and Suetonius, which they say happened at Cæsar's landing, we have no reason to conclude that Plutarch's story is to be referred to the time of his landing; in fact, it would be more natural to conclude that it occurred when he was crossing the Thames, or some other river. Supposing, however, that Plutarch did relate *the same* story as Valerius and Suetonius, let us estimate the value of his testimony. In the first place, he wrote one hundred years after Cæsar's invasion of Britain, and his knowledge of the event must have been derived from Cæsar's own narrative, or from other traditionary accounts, so that his testimony is not that of an eye-witness, or even of a contemporary of Cæsar. Again, the title he gives to his writings—"Plutarch's Lives"—sufficiently indicates their aim and scope, and shows that he intended rather to present the histories and characters of his heroes, than to give a detailed account of the events of the times in which they lived. To this end he arranged his "Lives" in pairs, each pair containing the life of a Greek and of a Roman hero. Julius Cæsar's life, for example, he compares with that of Alexander, pointing out the points of similarity in their characters and career. While, therefore, we should expect to find him writing with accuracy with respect to Cæsar's personal history, Plutarch would not be careful to enquire into the truth of every story related of his soldiers. A few years before he wrote, Aulus Plautius had landed in Britain, and his landing had been unopposed, the Britons hiding themselves in marshes and woods, in order to entice his army into dangerous and inextricable places. Such a report reaching the ears of

Plutarch, might very well lead him to conclude that the southern shore of Britain was everywhere marshy, and to place the scene of the noble deed of Scæva in the mire and marsh rather than among the sand and rocks of the ocean.

The other testimony adduced by Batteley is that of Dion Cassius. He states that Cæsar "having sailed round a certain promontory, landed on the other side, and there scattered the enemy who attacked him when landing his army in the marshes (τα τεναγη), and occupied the ground." Now, it is probable that Dion Cassius, who wrote a century later than Plutarch, and therefore about two hundred years after the time of Julius Cæsar, was led into error by the same cause as Plutarch, or perhaps through following his account of Scæva's exploit. It must be observed, however, that his description is not altogether inconsistent with Cæsar's narrative, since τα τεναγη imply generally muddy or shifting ground, but *not necessarily* marshes. Nor is it by any means certain that the shore of Deal would not at the time of Cæsar's landing have given occasion for some such description, the beach which now bounds the shore having probably been thrown up at a subsequent period.

In his zeal for Rutupium our learned author, Archdeacon Batteley, makes the most of these quotations from Plutarch and Dion Cassius, because they afford his only argument against Cæsar's landing having taken place at Deal; his other objections to Deal being in reality only apologies for his own departure from this traditional landing-place.

Let us consider his further arguments, or rather apologies, for his choice of Rutupium.

He first endeavours to meet the objection that Richborough is sixteen miles from Dover, whereas Cæsar states that his landing-place was only eight Roman miles from the place where he first approached the shore. Batteley, recognising how well Dover suits Cæsar's description of the latter place, suggests that the reading of eight miles may be inaccurate. This may doubtless have been the case, since the manuscripts generally state seven miles to have been the distance (which would tell still more against his argument), and it is not improbable that vii may have been by some transcribers changed into viii. But apart from this slight error, which may easily have crept in, it is not likely that the distance given by Cæsar has been altered, no writings of antiquity having been more carefully preserved than those of Cæsar, owing to the attention given to literature in the Augustan age, which succeeded him. Batteley further suggests that the Romans, in common with other ancient nations, were inexperienced in the art of measuring distances by sea, and that Cæsar therefore probably erred in the calculation of the distance he had travelled. Now, it is hardly possible that he could have travelled sixteen miles to Richborough, and imagined he had only sailed seven miles, even had he been thus inexperienced in calculating distances by sea. But he had no need to trust to his own judgment of the distance. When at last he had effected a landing, and defeated the Britons, Comius, the Atrebatian, whom the Britons had imprisoned, was restored to him. Comius knew the coast well, and could give certain information as to the distance by land from Dover to the place of landing, so that Cæsar had abundant opportunity of verifying his own reckoning. It must also be remembered that the Britons travelled by land to prevent his disembarkation, and that since Cæsar, after loosing his vessels from Dover, sailed with the wind and tide both in his favour, sixteen miles would have been an almost impossible distance for them to have travelled, in time to anticipate and oppose his landing.

Batteley, however, realising that facts are against him in his attempt to reconcile the distance between Dover and Richborough with that recorded in "the Commentaries," changes his argument, and attempts to throw doubts upon Dover being the place intended by Cæsar. "It is to no purpose," he says, "to state that Cæsar sought to land at the port of Dover, since there are other places on that shore no less difficult of approach than Dover on account of the rocks." "Where are the places?" we may ask. To suit Batteley's purpose they must be much nearer to Richborough than Dover is; but with the exception of the small inlet called St Margaret's Bay, which we have no reason to believe was ever a port, there is no other place at all answering to the description. Dover, as we have seen, answers to it perfectly.

Further, with reference to the statement of Dion Cassius, that Cæsar sailed round a certain promontory before he reached his place of disembarkation, Archdeacon Batteley remarks, "there was a promontory near Rutupium, which being sailed round, a port is reached, such as Cæsar required, suitable for a multitude of large vessels." But he explains that "the promontory was not the Pepernesse of to-day, but the extreme boundary of the shore, wherever it was, and by whatsoever name it was known, which was on the left of those entering the Rutupian harbour, and which now perhaps is a considerable distance from the sea." Standing on the hill of Richborough we look around and wonder where this promontory could have been, for Richborough itself is on the highest ground for some miles round, and no signs of a promontory of any kind present themselves in the direction whence Cæsar would have come. How indefinite and indeed imaginary is such a supposed promontory, compared with that which is circumnavigated by vessels sailing from Dover to Deal, called the South Foreland. The abruptness of this promontory is not very noticeable on the map of the coast, but to one coasting along, as Cæsar did, near the shore round its rugged and projecting rocks, Dion Cassius needs no justification in calling it a "promontory," or the Dover boatmen of the present day in speaking of it as "the point."

One advantage claimed by Batteley for Rutupium we readily concede, namely, that its harbour afforded far safer anchorage for vessels than the open shore of Deal, unless moored at some distance from the land. This alone would, I think, of itself be conclusive against the statement that Cæsar landed at Rutupium. For how could that be a safe anchorage, where his vessels were, on each occasion, driven on shore and wrecked? Deal certainly was not a port, and although it afforded ample room for Cæsar to land his troops, which was apparently what he chiefly thought of, the event proved that there was no safe anchorage for his vessels close to the shore. Had he landed at Richborough, as Batteley contends, his vessels would probably have been perfectly safe from the storms which wrecked them.

How, then, can we agree with the following argument by which our learned author concludes his remarks respecting Cæsar's landing-place. "I may say, in a word, that the Romans, during the whole time in which they possessed our island, landed at the Portus Rutupinus only, and unless anything can be shown to the contrary, I conclude that Cæsar there disembarked, and that others after Cæsar, led by his example, landed at the same place." We say, on the contrary, that the disasters he met with on each occasion of his invasion of Britain in the destruction of his fleet, served as beacons to warn others against attempting to land upon the same shore. We find, accordingly, that no attempt was made to land at Deal by those who subsequently invaded our country. Richborough and its safe harbour, commanding the nearest approach by sea to London, became, as Batteley correctly asserts, the place of disembarkation of future conquerors, and a place of arms during the Roman occupation of Britain.

www.ingramcontent.com/pod-product-compliance
Lightning Source LLC
Chambersburg PA
CBHW021358230426

43666CB00006B/564